Top of the Pops: 1964-2002

1964-2002

Jeff Simpson

It's still Number One, it's Top of the Pops!

Top of the Pops: The True Story was produced by Jeff
Simpson and Eliot Johnson and was first broadcast on
BBC1 in January 2001.
Executive Producer: Chris Cowey
Published by BBC Worldwide Ltd, 80 Wood Lane,
London W12 0TT
First published 2002
© Jeff Simpson 2002
The moral right of the author has been asserted.

ISBN 0 563 53476 1

Commissioning Editor: Emma Shackleton
Project Editor: Sarah Lavelle
Picture Researcher: Claire Parker
Copy Editor: Kate Quarry
Cover Art Director: Pene Parker
Book Designer: Lisa Pettibone
Production Controller: Susan Currie

Set in Tarzana and Proforma
Printed and bound in Italy by L.E.G.O. spa
Colour separations by Kestrel Digital Colour, Chelmsford

contents

foreword

On 1 January 1964 at 6.35 p.m., a voice on BBC1 announced, 'It's Number One, it's *Top of the Pops*', cueing in a live music show from a converted church in Manchester. Thirty-eight years later, in August 2002, the same show clocked up its 2000th edition — introduced, as ever, by the words, 'It's *still* Number One...'. Today, of course, it all looks very different from that first ramshackle music show. But its simple appeal — of giving music fans a chance to check in on each week's pop chart — has always remained the same.

The journey, however, hasn't been an easy one. Week after week, the show has to deal with the unruly egos of pop stars, the might of record companies, and the fickle tastes of the record-buying public. And it has to keep up to date — to change and evolve, and still remain at the cutting edge of music and fashion, and of television itself. For the most part, it's done pretty well, but there have also been times when it's missed the mark completely, and unintentionally provided some of the most memorable moments in TV history.

Of course, this book will celebrate how *Top of the Pops* became a national institution — but it will also ask why the show sometimes got it wrong. And the answer is invariably because of the BBC itself. It's clear that despite creating this hugely successful show, the BBC has always somehow failed to recognize exactly what the magic of *Top of the Pops* actually is. Some of the best moments in this book are about what happened when a series of wild and rebellious rock 'n' rollers confronted the old-school, establishment BBC — and neither side quite knew how to deal with the other.

Producer Eliot Johnson and I interviewed dozens of former production staff, musicians, dancers, fans and music industry people for a BBC1 documentary called *Top of the Pops: The True Story*. With further interviews carried out especially for this book, the whole story can now be told — happily, with fantastic illustration too. Harry Goodwin took stunning backstage photos of all the acts from the first decade of the show. The BBC went on to wipe most of the performances, but thankfully, Harry saved his stills, and is allowing us to publish them for the first time in this book. I myself found a stash of never-before-seen photos from the seventies and eighties gathering dust in a drawer in the *Top of the Pops* office, which again have never been seen in public. In recent years, it's been the job of photographer Mark Allan to take official portraits of the stars in action, and his superb shots illustrate the latter parts of the book.

But the pictures, and this book as a whole, do not aim to represent the story of British pop music. This is the story of *Top of the Pops* itself. It's a celebration of the affection we all have for the programme, of its fantastic highs and hilarious lows. It's a look at what makes the show so special for generation after generation — and at why it will still be 'Number One' for generations to come.

Jeff Simpson

1960s

Think of the sixties, and dozens of different images flash into your mind. Now think how many of those images come from *Top of the Pops*: Mick Jagger strutting and pouting in front of the cameras; polished girl groups like The Supremes, hippies like Sonny and Cher; Carnaby Street fashions — mini-skirts, high boots and false eyelashes; 'cool cat' presenters like Jimmy Savile, Alan 'Fluff' Freeman and Tony Blackburn. They were all right there on *Top of the Pops*. In the sixties, the show was the window through which the nation watched 'happenings' happen. Week after week, *Top of the Pops* brought the looks and sounds of the Swinging Sixties straight into our living rooms. The dads were saying, 'Call that music?', while the mums checked out the fashions, and the kids grooved along to the tunes — one way or another, the whole family was mesmerized by the show.

Above: Jimmy Savile, presenter of the first *Top of the Pops*. Below: Diana Ross, photographed at the show in October 1964. Opposite, top: The Hollies, at the first show in January 1964. Opposite, main: The audience became stars from show one.

Right: The studio in Dickenson Road, Manchester, in May 1965, as Jimmy Savile prepares to introduce that week's Number One from Sandie Shaw.
Opposite: The *Top of the Pops* chart rundown in May 1965.

The Swinging Sixties

In the sixties, *Top of the Pops* was the one programme where you could see a phenomenon rare to TV in those days: Young People. With hindsight, we know that the sixties were the time to be young and a music fan, but the BBC certainly didn't know it at the time. The Corporation *suffered Top of the Pops*, even though (or perhaps because) it was the only regular slot where young people had a platform that was free from that patronizing 'Auntie Beeb' tone. On *Top of the Pops* a young audience could see kids living lives that were utterly different from those of their parents.

According to those sixties icons, Pan's People, two things defined the outlook of young people at the time – the Pill and the Bomb. The first allowed women sexual liberation, the chance to take control of their own lives in a way they had never been able to before. The second made them feel they might not even be around to see the seventies. So Pan's People danced. They lived life to the full, danced every week on *Top of the Pops* and became stars.

But it wasn't just Pan's People who discovered that *Top of the Pops* worked a certain kind of magic on those who appeared: the bands, too, soon realized it was more than a commercial showcase – it was an occasion, a party, one of the perks of being a pop star. Even the audience became stars on *Top of the Pops*, showing off their fashions and dance moves, and hoping their friends would spot them on TV. In the sixties, *Top of the Pops* had a magic all of its own, and here's how it started.

Inventing a show

It was 1963, and London was starting to swing to a brand new beat. Thanks to bands like The Beatles, The Hollies, The Rolling Stones, Gerry & The Pacemakers and The Searchers, rock 'n' roll now belonged to Britain and to a new generation of teenagers.

At the end of 1963 a young graduate called Jim Moir found himself in the imposing Art Deco reception of the BBC's Broadcasting House in central London. He was there for an interview for the post of trainee producer in a department known as Light Entertainment.

That December morning, he had to face the legendary Tom Sloan, a Reithian icon, best described as the entertainments officer to the nation. It was Sloan who had Britain singing along to *The Good Old Days* and shouting 'Boom boom!' at Basil Brush. This was an era when the BBC had banned 'inappropriate' material in comedy routines, including lines like 'winter draws [drawers] on' and references to 'travelling salesmen'.

Now controller of Radio 2, Jim remembers the interview as a terrifying experience. 'But I was determined to pitch in with my idea,' he recalls. Jim was going to suggest doing a programme about the new British music scene, which had become so vibrant throughout 1963. 'At the time, British pop music had become absolutely dominant, so I said I thought the BBC should be carrying a pop show, featuring the great successes of British music. As I gave my brilliant exposition of this programme, Tom Sloan held his hand up and said, "Well, Mr Moir, just in case you should ever think that we stole your idea, I should tell you that we in Light Entertainment Group already have a similar show in mind."' The BBC brat that became known as *Top of the Pops* had already been conceived.

The head of Variety for the Corporation at the time was Bill Cotton, son of the celebrated bandleader Billy Cotton. Bill Jr had made music shows like *Off the Record*, *Six-Five Special* and *Juke Box Jury*. Now he'd been given an important task – to counter the growing success of commercial television. 'The BBC had done good things in popular music,'

explains Cotton, 'but then along came *Ready, Steady, Go!* on ITV, and they became top dog. It got good figures, very, very good. The man who was in charge of BBC1 called me in and said, "These figures for *Ready, Steady, Go!* are very high, and you can't even get a show to match it." I was rather bruised. But at the weekend, I went home and thought about it.'

Over that weekend Bill Cotton invented *Top of the Pops*. 'What struck me,' he says, 'was that the majority of the hit parade was British. Previously, it had been mostly American. But now, out of the Top 20, there were probably 15 or 16 British songs. Why didn't we do a hit parade show? So I put the idea forward, and I think we did a deal for half-a-dozen shows.' Cotton had spotted the time was exactly right for a *British* music show. One of the top UK bands was The Hollies and singer Allan Clarke says the timing was perfect: 'Suddenly the buzz started. There seemed to be a million groups from Liverpool, a million groups from Manchester, all putting their own mark on the British scene.'

'Suddenly the buzz started. There seemed to be a million groups from Liverpool, a million groups from Manchester, all putting their own mark on the British scene.' ALLAN CLARKE

programme was to go out live on New Year's Day 1964. The first job was to find a frontman. 'I decided to have a different presenter every week,' says Stewart. 'I chose Jimmy Savile for the first one, because I thought he was a fun guy. He already had a show on Radio Luxembourg called *Teen and 20 Record Club*.' The others were Alan Freeman, who was on radio with *Pick of the Pops*, David Jacobs from *Juke Box Jury*, and Pete Murray from *Six-Five Special*.

Top of the Pops' new offices were at Television Centre in west London – so the entire team had to decamp and head north on the train for the broadcast. They were in no way prepared for the sight that greeted them outside the old church. The Beatles were Number One that week with 'I Wanna Hold Your Hand', and an army of young female fans was besieging the studio. 'There was a great crowd of young people outside because pop stars were coming,' says Jimmy Savile. 'It was just an almighty heave-ho outside. There was heave-ho inside as well, and it was all live but nobody was bothered because we didn't know any better anyway.'

The Beatles' fans were disappointed – the lads were on the programme, but only on film. The show, however, did feature The Rolling Stones, Dusty Springfield, The Hollies, The Dave Clark Five and The Swinging Blue Jeans.

The first programme

Allan Clarke was on the first *Top of the Pops* with The Hollies. 'When I saw that it was an old church, it deflated me a bit. How can you get rock 'n' roll in a church? But when we walked in, we all changed our minds because there was Jimmy Savile, who we'd known for quite a long time. And there were a lot of other faces we knew from the rock 'n' roll world – like Dusty and The Swinging Blue

Top: The clean-cut Rolling Stones, seen here at the first *Top of the Pops*, January 1964.
Above: The BBC's Northern Studios, a converted church in Dickenson Road, Manchester, where the first *Top of the Pops* was made.

The new show, which Cotton christened *Top of the Pops*, was to be made in Manchester. Much of the music itself came from northern England and the BBC's Northern Studios were already the home of more typical variety shows like Val Doonican's. But there's little doubt that one of the main reasons the programme was based in Manchester was because of the 'moral panic' about pop music that had gripped the Establishment. BBC bosses certainly didn't want all those dangerous, scruffy musicians messing up their smart new Television Centre in London. In fact, the grandly titled Northern Studios were based in a converted church in Manchester's Dickenson Road. The pews had been removed to create the studio floor, the gallery was in what had been the choir, and the dressing rooms were cobbled together out of former vestries. This was the humble birthplace of *Top of the Pops*.

Cotton chose as producer Johnnie Stewart, a well-spoken former radio man who'd cut his teeth on shows like *Juke Box Jury*. The launch

Jeans. It was like everyone was going to have a party. I remember first seeing the board at the back with that week's Top 40 on it. Jimmy was at a table in front of it. Our song was quite low to the bottom, and I was saying to myself, I hope Jimmy doesn't stand in front of it or no one will see where we are in the chart. But Johnnie Stewart gave us the feeling that we were here to have fun. I think that showed on most of the early shows on *Top of the Pops*, that everybody was there for a good time.'

The show went live on air at 6.35 p.m. on New Year's Day, opening with the words, 'It's Number One, it's *Top of the Pops*'.

FIRST
TOP OF THE POPS

Manchester, 1 January 1964
Presenter: Jimmy Savile

Live in the studio
Rolling Stones 'I Wanna Be Your Man'
The Hollies 'Stay'
Dusty Springfield 'I Only Want To Be With You'
Swinging Blue Jeans 'Hippy Hippy Shake'
Dave Clark Five 'Glad All Over'
Audience dancing to Gene Pitney '24 Hours from Tulsa'
Film sequences of
Freddie & the Dreamers 'You Were Made For Me'
The Beatles 'I Wanna Hold Your Hand' (news footage)
Plus live insert from
Alan Freeman in London

▶▶ Keith Richards

The Rolling Stones were on the first *Top of the Pops*, and remained regulars on the show.

We were on the road, playing in Aberystwyth the night before that first *Top of the Pops*. Our road manager shoved us in the back of our little pink Volkswagen van with no windows. Basically the equipment took up the room and then you just shoved the band in around it. Oh, we're on TV, great, *Top of the Pops*.

Somehow we arrived at this complex in Manchester, and nobody knows what's happening, nobody. The crew were all there tripping over each other. It was a great ramshackle event at the beginning, 'cos everyone was making it up as they went along. It wasn't like *Juke Box Jury*, where everybody had to sit down and do what they were told. Everybody was kind of feeling their way.

Then there'd be Jimmy [Savile] ... 'More peroxide, Jim? It's going off a bit round the back.' It was his energy that really did keep it together. He'd keep popping in and out going, 'All right boys, all right?' He energized the whole thing before the show went out.

The real fun of *Top of the Pops* was not doing the show. It was backstage that was really funny. You'd find all these things in the dressing rooms. You'd get to your dressing room, open up the drawer — ooh, look who's left half a bottle of vodka, or some weed. So the first thing is the dressing room, and then the actual doing of the show. We were actually very good boys

backstage, compared to some.

For one *Top of the Pops*, we were on the bill with — what was his name? — Craig Douglas, the singing milkman from the Isle of Wight. So we promptly left, like, a little note with some bottles outside his dressing room saying, 'Three pints, please'.

On *Top of the Pops*, you're miming, you're lip synching. It's kind of harder to mime or lip synch to something than it is to actually just play live, because you have to remember to match to the record. On the road you're doing it for real, and then for the TV show you've got to remember what the hell you played when you first recorded it. You're going, 'I hope they don't recognize my mouth not moving in the wrong spot.'

But that was the way you promoted your record in those days. After all, this was the days of 45s where you needed a new one every two months. And *Top of the Pops* provided the perfect outlet for that. In a way, for a government agency, it was quite commercial.

There was something about *Top of the Pops*, it's something to do with the Beeb, really. I grew up with the BBC, I listened to it, I believed in it fervently, so working with the BBC, you know, there was something extra.

So, *Top of the Pops* is still going? Bloody hell! I might come back on — if I can come up with a good song!

TOP OF THE POPS

Right: Dusty Springfield appeared on the first *Top of the Pops*, with 'I Only Want To Be With You'.

Making an impact

No tapes exist of the first programme, but there's no doubt it had an instant impact. The six-week run was extended and the show quickly became beloved by the crew, the bands and the mainly young viewers. But it wasn't an easy ride. There were advantages to being in Manchester, where the programme could do its own thing away from interfering BBC bosses, but the location meant there were continual problems booking acts, especially during the winter. There was no M6 yet, and the airport was often fog-bound. Sometimes only a couple of band members would turn up, and missing ones were replaced by stand-ins from other bands. It was not unknown to have The Animals on, with Eric Burdon at the front, and a backline made up of a couple of Kinks and a

Who, all disguised by shadowy lighting. Often, a band wouldn't turn up at all, and the director was left with no choice but to shoot the audience dancing along to the number. This was the start of the audience gradually becoming the unsung star of *Top of the Pops*.

During the harsh winter of 1965–6, Allan Clarke had the most challenging journey of his life to get to the show. 'I was heading off in the car from London to Manchester to do *Top of the Pops*,' he recalls, 'and it started snowing, and it snowed and snowed. Hours later, I was stranded near Tamworth in huge drifts of snow. Somehow, I managed to get to the nearest station, which was Crewe, and got a train which was going to get into Manchester Piccadilly at 7.20 ... and the programme was going to start at 7.25. Live. Of course, the rest

1	I WANT TO HOLD YOUR HAND The Beatles
2	GLAD ALL OVER The Dave Clark Five
3	SHE LOVES YOU The Beatles
4	YOU WERE MADE FOR ME Freddie & The Dreame
5	I ONLY WANT TO BE WITH YOU Dusty Springfield
6	'24 HOURS FROM TULSA Gene Pitney
	DOMINIQUE The Singing Nun
8	SECRET LOVE Kathy Kirby
9	SWINGIN' ON A STAR Big Dee Irwin
10	HIPPY HIPPY SHAKE Swinging Blue Jeans
11	MARIA ELENA Los Indios Tabajaras
12	DON'T TALK TO HIM Cliff Richard
13	I WANNA BE YOUR MAN The Rolling Stones
14	THE BEATLES (L.P.) The Beatles

of the band didn't know where I was. So I'm on this train and all of a sudden I hear, "What are you doing, Clarky?" And it was Brian Jones [of The Rolling Stones]. He was also doing the show. I said, "Brian, we're going to be late, we should get changed on the train." I was travelling in dirty jeans, a shirt and a jerkin, and he had a three-piece suit on. So I went into to the toilet and came out in his three-piece suit, and he came out of the toilet in my dirty jeans, shirt and jerkin. That was our different images, you see. He said, "Right, we're ready to rock 'n' roll!" We got to Piccadilly station at 7.20 and jumped straight into a cab, which drove on the pavement to get us there in time. Thank God I wasn't the first on.'

There was never any pretence about artists miming on *Top of the Pops*. The presenters were

Right: Jimmy Savile with the chart rundown at the first show. His job was to spin the discs, so that artists could mime along to the records.

▸▸ Jimmy Savile

Jimmy Savile presented the very first *Top of the Pops***, and continued as a presenter of the show for 18 years.**

I got a call from Johnnie Stewart: 'My name's Johnnie Stewart, I'm working on *Top of the Pops*, can you work with me on it?' And we had six weeks to put the show together. That's really how it started. In those days, older people dictated what younger people could do, but suddenly there was this great surge where younger people started to pressurize and demand certain things, amongst which was pop music. *Top of the Pops* was a sop for this pop culture, which was forcing itself onto older people. It was sop so that the BBC could say, yes of course we look after young people 'cos look at this 'Top of the Paps' or 'Pop of the Tips' or whatever it was called. So really it just happened to be there by sufferance. It was just a passing phase, or so the BBC thought. But we made it a household name.

It was the only show where parents could sit down and join in with something with their kids. And the kids could opinionate and tell their parents about this, that and the other. *Top of the Pops* epitomized what was going on for younger people at the time, and it was called the Swinging Sixties. It was simple, insofar as most things were safe, sex was safe. Booze hadn't

raised its head to the extent it has today. Drugs were practically non-existent. It was such a time of freedom and emancipation for young people and everything was wonderful, and *Top of the Pops* mirrored that.

I said to Johnnie Stewart, 'Mark my words, the audience will be as important as the groups.' Bearing in mind that I made a big fuss of the audience, I made sure the audience got just as much camera coverage as the groups did, 'cos I considered the audience, if anything, more important than the groups. And you could see from the way they behaved that it was a perfectly natural demonstration of trouble-free joy. They were so appreciative of coming to *Top of the Pops* for free, and cheek by jowl with these amazing groups that they were in touching distance of. So that atmosphere created by the audience reflected onto the groups and the groups loved being with the audience. They weren't on a programme, they were part of a programme.

I loved being on *Top of the Pops* because it was part of the fabric of my existence. I was doing my own *Top of the Pops* before *Top of the Pops* was invented. So when *Top of the Pops* came along I only carried on being me.

TOP OF THE POPS

Above: Jim with Mike Nesmith and Micky Dolenz of The Monkees, trying on Mike's famous woolly hat. They were appearing on the same show as Jimi Hendrix and The Four Tops.

used like DJs, and were always seen putting the needle on the record as they introduced the band. For a while, the role of cueing the disc was given to a pretty model called Samantha Juste, who became known as 'the putter-onner'. She became a star in her own right, and later married Micky Dolenz of the Monkees, whom she met backstage on the programme.

Occasionally, the miming looked a little strange – for example, when P.J. Proby, a huge heart-throb at the time, was pulled off stage into the crowd. He could occasionally be seen coming up for air, still bravely trying to mouth the words to his song. Generally, though, none of the bands seemed to mind having to mime – for many, it was a chance to relax and have a drink before the show in the Wellcome Inn next door, without having to worry about the performance. For the viewers the issue of miming never seemed to matter either. The attraction of *Top of the Pops* was that you could see the faces of the artists whose records you were buying. As long as the stars were up there on screen, very few viewers even thought about whether they were actually singing.

The Manchester years saw four very different presenters as regular hosts. There was the energetic Alan 'Fluff' Freeman, a big star in the early sixties, who earned his nickname

because of his regular gaffes (his most famous was introducing the song 'Cast Your Fate to the Wind' as 'Cast Your Wind to the Fate'). David Jacobs was another regular, a rather dignified and avuncular figure with the tone of a typical BBC announcer. And there was Pete Murray, a man with a slightly 'cooler' outlook, who tried hard to act as a big-brother figure to the young viewers. But the real star was Jimmy Savile. 'Savile was the only one who wasn't patronizing,' says another of the show's producers, Stan Dorfman. 'He understood the audience, he was like a kid himself, he behaved like a kid, and the audience could relate to him.' Jacobs wore a suit, Murray sported the occasional leather jacket, and 'Fluff' wore his fluffy jumpers. But Savile stood out in zebra stripes, flowery patterns and, of course, his trademark jewellery. Jim's biggest mark on the show was to involve the studio audience. He'd ask them where they were from, whether they liked the bands and let them say 'hi' to their mums. He knew that viewers loved the idea that members of the audience could be stars.

Savile became a towering presence on *Top of the Pops* – he set the tone for the programme, and continued to front it until 1981. But no one who worked with him ever really understood the man himself. 'He was an enigma,' says Dorfman. 'You'd never know what he was thinking, because he was performing all the time. He lived in a caravan, which he'd bring to the show. He'd go off and wrestle at the weekends. [Yes, he was a professional wrestler, too.] Then he'd go off and work in a hospital. He had this whole element of giving. He could talk about football and politics, he'd talk about his mother a lot, but you never got any emotion. He certainly never talked about music. I don't think he ever listened to the music at home. But it didn't matter, because he was what he was.'

The magic formula

The Top 40 was – and still is – the key to *Top of the Pops*. People tuned in each week to see how their favourite stars and tunes were doing. 'It was a competition,' says Dorfman. 'It was like a sporting event, it kept you wanting to see it next week.' But it didn't take the music industry long to spot that an appearance on *Top of the Pops* had a direct and massive effect on sales and chart positions. The Top 40 was co-sponsored by the BBC, along with magazines like *NME* and *Melody Maker*, but at the same time, *Top of the Pops* couldn't be seen to influence the chart or favour particular artists. So Johnnie Stewart devised a set of rules: he decreed that anyone who was going up the chart could be featured, anyone who was going down could not. Nobody should appear two weeks running, apart from the Number One, which always ended the show. Exactly the same formula is still at the heart of the show today.

But Stewart's rules also created problems for the production team, because the chart was announced on a Tuesday lunchtime, and the show had to be ready for Thursday or, later on, a Wednesday-night taping. 'We'd have our draft running order ready, and we'd wait on tenterhooks,' says Dorfman 'We'd have everything pencilled in, then we'd get the charts and have to change it all.'

Over the first two years the show welcomed stars like Chuck Berry, The Everly Brothers, Joan Baez, The Supremes, Sonny and Cher and The Byrds. 'It had all these amazing artists on, but at that point, nobody knew they were amazing,' says Dorfman. 'Never have there been line-ups like we had then.' Sonny and Cher caused wonder and confusion when they arrived at Dickenson Road in the summer of 1965 to perform 'I Got You Babe'. They were the first hippies to appear on the show, and astounded many with their California tans, headbands, furry jackets, and message of Peace and Love. When producers first heard the record, they wrote a camera script assuming the deep voice was Sonny, and the high voice was Cher. When they performed, it was the other way round, and the script had to be torn up.

BBC bosses left this ramshackle little pop show to its own devices: to them, it was a slightly distasteful show made in Manchester in a converted church with three cameras, mad hosts, and a bunch of weird pop stars. But it was for kids, so they could live with it. Then something happened.

Below: Sonny and Cher photographed at one of three appearances promoting 'I Got You Babe' in the summer of 1965.

The move to London

At the start of 1966, *Top of the Pops* moved to London, and a whole new era began. By the time the decision to move was made, the programme had grown and grown, delivering 20 million viewers a week for BBC1. The production team was tired with commuting to Dickenson Road every week and with the constant problems of getting bands up to Manchester. But the main reason it moved – on 20 January 1966 – wasn't because of the crew, or the artists, or even the BBC itself. It was because the Musicians' Union decided that having all these acts miming on TV was putting their members out of work; the BBC didn't want to fall out with the MU, as it would threaten all their radio and TV entertainment shows. *Top of the Pops* could easily have been taken off air at this point, swatted out of the schedule by a powerful union. But if there was one thing the BBC hated more than pop music, it was being dictated to by the unions. A bold decision was made: if they wanted live music on *Top of the Pops*, they'd get live music. An orchestra was formed that could re-create virtually any tune; soloists like Lulu or Tom Jones would sing to the orchestra, and full bands would play live.

Manchester was too small to house a live orchestra, so the whole show was hauled down south to Television Centre. Just as London was starting to swing.

The new *Top of the Pops* was instantly bigger and better. Gone was the makeshift 'let's do the show right here' atmosphere of Dickenson Road. 'In Manchester, it was pretty much a teeny-bopper-type show,' says Dorfman, who oversaw the move for Johnnie Stewart. 'When it moved to London it became chic, it became stylish. The budget went up and we started getting these magnificent sets. We had London designers, people who'd come out of the Royal Academy. There was a designer called Roger Lowe, who was a huge innovator and did tremendous sets with metal cages and movement. Also, it became this big social event every week. Everyone would turn up to the taping and, of course, to the bar afterwards.'

It wasn't just the set where the viewers noticed the difference: suddenly, all the great acts like Dusty Springfield and The Stones, were singing live on the show, putting in real performances. 'It became a real rock 'n' roll show,' adds Dorfman. 'And the age of the studio audience went up from 13 and 14, to 18, 19, 20.' One particularly memorable show on 18 January 1967 featured The Four Tops, Cat Stevens, The Monkees and Alan Price, as well as the legendary Jimi Hendrix. Dorfman remembers Hendrix as 'a very quiet, very delicate man who did get upset about things. He used to throw up before the show, he was so nervous. But once he got on stage, he was Hendrix, of course.'

Whatever the band, *Top of the Pops* provided a visual feast each and every week. As London got into full swing, the show became a weekly window into 'where it's at'. Britain was leading the world in fashion, with names like Biba, Vidal Sassoon and Mary Quant, and

---

FIRST PROGRAMME FROM LONDON

20 January 1966

Presenter: David Jacobs (Studio 2, Television Centre)

Cilla Black 'Love's Just a Broken Heart'

Otis Redding 'My Girl'

Paul and Barry Ryan 'Have Pity on the Boy'

David and Jonathan 'Michelle'

Crispian St Peters 'You Were On My Mind'

Herman's Hermits 'A Must To Avoid'

Stevie Wonder 'Uptight'

Film sequence of Herb Alpert 'Spanish Flea'

Spencer Davis Group 'Keep On Running' (Number One)

Left: The Beach Boys' Mike
Love (l) and Bruce Johnston
(r) with *Top of the Pops*
producer Johnnie Stewart
(centre l) and director
Brian Whitehouse (centre r).
Below: Eyebrows were
raised, as well as hem-
lines, when the first
mini-skirts appeared.

although Carnaby Street and the King's Road
were in London, the whole nation could check
out the latest looks every week on *Top of the
Pops*. There were rumours that Mary Quant
sent models to infiltrate the audience wearing
her gear. Producers knew the value of the new
fashions as well – crew members were sent
out to clubs like The Revolution, Scotts of St
James and the Cromwellian to give out tickets
– but only to the coolest cats and chicks. In
fact, tickets to the show became like gold dust.
Pete Murray found clear evidence of the
demand: 'I was stopped in the street one day
by a well-dressed woman, who asked if I could
get her a couple of tickets for *Top of the Pops*. I
tried to get myself out of it by saying, "I don't
know, it's not all that easy." She said, "Well I
have to be perfectly honest with you, I'm a
prostitute and I'll give you a freebie if you give
me the tickets."'

Whatever their profession, the audience was
encouraged to dress up when prizes were
awarded for the best dressed person and the
best dancer (the prize was the Top 10 singles,
but the real reward was to be featured on
camera). Producers were so conscious of how it
all looked that they had to take one of the crew
in hand, floor manager Cecil Korer, whose
shiny bald head kept popping up on camera in
amongst the hippies. Cecil was obliged to wear
a BBC wig during the show so that he didn't
stand out from the trendy crowd.

The acts, of course, would not be outdone
by the audience, or by other bands. Lulu
remembers, 'You had to wear something that
was really hip on *Top of the Pops*, 'cos everybody was looking at everyone else's outfits.' In
they came, band after band with guys in sharp
suits or flower-power shirts, and girl singers in
mini-skirts, boots, geometric-patterned dresses
and that distinctive heavy eye make-up.

'You had to wear something that was really hip on *Top of the Pops*, 'cos everybody was looking at everyone else's outfits.' LULU

Top: Lulu was 15 when she made her debut on *Top of the Pops*. Later, she met her first husband, Maurice Gibb, backstage at the show.
Above: The Bee Gees at the Christmas show in 1967, when they performed 'Massachusetts'.

By 1967 the show was enjoying a golden era. The Christmas show that year featured The Rolling Stones, The Bee Gees, Procol Harum, Lulu, Cliff Richard and the famous film of The Beatles' 'All You Need Is Love'.

The same year saw another injection of new blood. Radio 1 started in September 1967, and soon the groovy young DJs were bringing their own style to *Top of the Pops*. It was a chance for the audience to put faces to the famous names. Simon Dee presented *Top of the Pops* around this time, as did Emperor Rosko and Kenny Everett. But the most famous of them all was Tony Blackburn. His Radio 1 breakfast show had made him a huge star at the tender age of 21 (that's if you believe the press release). 'The combination of Radio 1 and *Top of the Pops* made me into a national name,' he says. 'What did *Top of the Pops* do for me? It made it impossible for me to go to the fish and chip shop!'

Of course, the show was doing the same job for the parade of stars that came through its doors. 'It was definitely a mark that you'd made it,' says Rick Parfitt of Status Quo,

whose debut was with 'Pictures of Matchstick Men' in February 1968. The Quo at that time were a far cry from the pony-tailed rockers we came to know and love. They were fresh-faced youths with fringes and satin frock-coats – and huge smiles. 'If you look back at the old footage,' says Francis Rossi, 'I've got this permanent grin on my face. I'm just knocked out to be there – on telly, pop star, fantastic.'

There was every reason to smile backstage as well, as the BBC bar became the focus of attention after the show, with producers and stars all swinging and rubbing shoulders with London's bright young things and getting drunk at record-company expense. It was here that Lulu met her first husband: 'I'd heard from my friend Joanna, who was Brian Epstein's secretary, that one of the little Bee Gees fancied me,' she says. 'I wondered, "Which one, which one?", because I thought they were all cute. And of course I met up with them at *Top of the Pops*, and that was the beginning of my romance which subsequently ended up in marriage to Maurice Gibb.'

Beatles and Stones

Top of the Pops had unique relationships with the two biggest groups of the sixties, The Beatles and The Rolling Stones. The Stones had been great friends of the show ever since that first programme in Dickenson Road, and they appeared more or less whenever they had a single out. But The Beatles were different. Even from that very first programme, when the Fab Four were Number One with 'I Wanna Hold Your Hand', it was clear that the hysteria known as 'Beatlemania' would prevent them from appearing live. When the programme became a hit, The Beatles' manager Brian Epstein called Bill Cotton to ask if 'the lads' could appear. The request was turned down on grounds of security. Instead, a compromise was reached that continued throughout The Beatles' career: they would make special films to be shown on the programme. Their road manager at the time was Tony Bramwell. 'We knew it was a powerful programme from day one,' he says, 'so we decided it would be useful to set time aside to do location shoots for Johnnie [Stewart]. Because of the safety prob-lems, we used to go to other BBC studios where they could go in and do things without fanmania or Beatlemania happening. We used to shoot them without an audience at the BBC Theatre or Lime Grove or the Riverside Studios, so that they could get there without the whole place being wrecked.'

One such recording took place on 16 June 1966. The day before, John, Paul, George and Ringo had recorded special films for EMI to be sent out worldwide to promote 'Paperback Writer' and 'Rain'. The films were needed immediately for that week's *Top of the Pops*, but they'd been recorded using the American format, and the BBC didn't have the facilities

Above: The Beatles came to the BBC's Lime Grove Studios on 16 June 1966 to record 'Paperback Writer' and 'Rain' for *Top of the Pops*. In the foreground (above, left), Beatles press officer Tony Burrows and manager Brian Epstein discuss the performance with the crew.

> ## TOP OF THE POPS BUDGET
> ### 3 January 1966
>
> **Presenter Alan Freeman** 150 guineas (£155, 50p)
> **The Beatles** 1000 pounds
> **Cilla Black** 131 pounds, 5s (shillings)
> **Marianne Faithfull** 52 pounds, 10s
> **Wayne Fontana** 26 pounds, 5s
> **Samantha Juste** (disc girl) 10 pounds, 10s

Above: Fresh Cream — a frizzy-haired Eric Clapton (left) on stage at *Top of the Pops* with Ginger Baker (centre) and Jack Bruce.

a new record out in the UK, so you'd say, "Is it all right if we send you a film clip?" It was basically primitive pop video. I think the Beatles and ourselves started that – without realizing what a bastard we'd brought into the world!'

The idea caught on quickly. When an act wasn't available, *Top of the Pops* often went out to shoot special films themselves, with many ground-breaking examples made by director Tom Taylor. The famous footage of Roy Orbison at the Roof Gardens in Kensington, singing 'Pretty Woman', is a classic example, shot because Roy couldn't make the studio date. Most of the films, though, were very simple, often featuring pretty girls walking around dreamily across fields. Occasionally they reflected the psychedelic mood of the times: The Hollies, for example, couldn't understand why, for their song 'Carrie Anne', a straightforward boy-meets-girl ditty, one band member had to dress in a skirt and run around Hampstead Heath, while another became a gun-slinger and a third was filmed surrounded by Playboy Bunnies. Ahh, the sixties!

Pan's People

Finally, then, as we move through this incredible decade when *Top of the Pops* embodied the most exciting spirit of the era, we turn to the dancers: Pan's People, icons of the age, who were created by the show itself.

To be fair, though, Pan's People weren't the first dance troupe to appear on *Top of the Pops*. Way back in Dickenson Road, choreographer Jo Cook created a three-girl group called The Go-Jos (a great sixties name, which could have come straight out of *Austin Powers*). The Go-Jos admirably fulfilled the role of providing a visual distraction by dancing along to the music of groups who couldn't make it to Manchester. When the show moved to London, there was much more space, and

to convert the tapes in time. The Beatles therefore went along to Lime Grove to re-record the two numbers especially for *Top of the Pops*. The budget for that week's programme shows that these one-off recordings were very costly for the programme, but at least it was a way of getting The Beatles on the show.

The Rolling Stones had been regulars on the show but, like The Beatles, they found themselves more and more in demand. So they, too, started shooting special films for *Top of the Pops*. It's a neglected part of pop history, but these films made for *Top of the Pops* were in fact the first pop videos. 'It was just that you couldn't be everywhere at once,' says Keith Richards. 'You'd be in Australia and you've got

three Go-Jos became six, with more elaborate costumes and routines. The Go-Jos also worked on Lulu's BBC1 show at the time. 'Mostly they wore those high white boots to the knee and short skirts,' she says, 'and the camera would always go right up the skirts. It was all very risqué.'

But although the routines were good, The Go-Jos were also in demand from other shows, including ITV. 'One time, we were on both channels at the same time,' confesses Jo Cook, 'so we didn't know which side to watch. Then Johnnie [Stewart] didn't ring me up any more, and one of the girls said, "Oh, Jo, there's another group of dancers on *Top of the Pops*." And that was the end of us.' Yes, *Top of the Pops* needed its very own stars – and boy, did they get stars.

Felicity 'Flick' Colby had arrived in London from New York during the cold winter of 1966. Trained at the Joffrey Ballet, she only went to dance classes in London as a way of keeping warm. There she hung out with other dancers, like Babs Lord, Ruth Pearson and Dee Dee Wilde. All three were 'Beat Girls', members of a group that appeared on a BBC2 music show, *The Beat Room* (produced by our old friend Jim Moir), and caused a scandal by appearing with bare midriffs. When Flick got a job as a Beat Girl, she was delighted – until she found out the series was about to end. Soon, like the rest of the girls, she found herself making ends meet by go-go dancing on top of a lighted drum in Soho nightclubs. She talked to Babs, Dee Dee and Ruth, and they decided to walk out on their manager and form their own group, along with two others, Louise Clarke and Andrea Rutherford, known as Andi.

Of course, they had defied convention by breaking away from their choreographer, so there was little work for them in British TV. They turned to the Continent, where TV

Above: As their outfits changed from frilly dresses to mini-skirts, boots and backcombed hair, *Top of the Pops* dancers Pan's People became icons of the Swinging Sixties.

Top: Pan's People (from left to right) — Flick Colby (choreographer), Dee Dee Wilde, Babs Lord, Ruth Pearson, Andi Rutherford and Louise Clarke.
Below: Jo Cook's Go-Jos were the first dance group on *Top of the Pops*.

stations in Belgium and Holland were trying out new 'artistic' forms of dance. 'We were going to call ourselves Dionysius Darlings,' says Flick, 'but I thought that was too hard for the Belgians to pronounce. So we became Pan's People [Pan being the god of dance]. We spent about a year working on the continent. I learned a lot and I made a lot of mistakes. But I also learned a lot of techniques for working with dancers on television – how to move the camera, how to do the lighting, all that kind of stuff. So then we did a very pretentious brochure about "the art of dance on TV", and we sent it out to every producer and director we could possibly think of. A guy called Colin Sharman, who worked on *Top of the Pops*, hired us to do one number.'

After that first appearance in April 1968, Pan's People became regulars, usually wearing dreamy, Laura Ashley-style outfits. But being true girls of the sixties, they couldn't resist the fashions of the day. According to Ruth, 'At the beginning, the BBC costume designer would be in charge of what we wore, and we often ended up in frilly numbers with daisies on them, which weren't suitable at all. Flick would actually design the outfits, and take them to the costume department to get them made. But as Flick got more and more in control, she was allowed to decide what we

wore. That's when it became more outrageous, more raunchy and generally more imaginative. And the sexier costumes were much easier to dance in.'

Costume wasn't the only area where Flick took control: she understood camera moves, and told the directors which shots she wanted, and when. The cameras themselves had to be choreographed, and that's exactly what she did. It must have been a great culture shock for the old-boy directors of the BBC to be faced with a sassy American girl, still in her early twenties, telling them where to point their cameras, but they knew it worked. As Flick took more control, she found it difficult to dance with the group at the same time as directing, so stepped behind the cameras as full-time choreographer. Hence, the classic five-piece line-up took shape and Britain fell in love with Pan's People.

However, there was one area Flick couldn't control – the music itself. Pan's People's job was to dance to the records when the artists weren't available, but if the chosen record dropped in the chart, they had to dance to something else. Often they had less than 24 hours to create a brand new routine. This is why our fondest memories of Pan's People probably include the slightly bizarre choreography. 'When you have six hours to create a

'...as Flick got more and more in control, she was allowed to decide what we wore. That's when it became more outrageous, more raunchy and generally more imaginative. And the sexier costumes were much easier to dance in.' RUTH PEARSON

routine, then that's what you have,' says Flick, philosophically. 'You had to make it work – which is why I'd like to take this opportunity to apologize and say I'm sorry if some of the routines didn't make sense, but that was what I was up against.'

Thankfully, though, the choreography was the last thing on the viewers' minds. Pan's People attracted different audiences for different reasons. The mums wanted to see the fashions, while the dads, of course, wanted the T & A (remember, there was no other show on TV at the time that featured pretty girls prancing about in hot pants or bikinis). And how many girls wanted to be members of Pan's People when they grew up? How many boys wanted to marry them? While Flick and her dancers took their art extremely seriously, they were in no doubt that their power lay in their sex appeal. 'We definitely used our sexuality to our advantage, particularly when it came to dealing with BBC bosses. In show-business,' she says, 'attractiveness is a commodity. We were very aware of what we had, and we used it.'

Unlike most dancers on TV, who appeared behind the star, Pan's People were the stars, and stars in their own right. People knew their names and had individual favourites. The most popular was the blonde and willowy Babs, known as 'Beautiful Babs'. She received thousands of letters a week, including many proposals of marriage. One director of the time, Stan Appel, remembers, 'If you were doing something off the cuff and said to the cameramen, hey guys, can I have a close-up of one of the girls? Suddenly, you'd get four or six cameras – vroom – all into Babs.'

Pan's People perfectly reflected the spirit of *Top of the Pops* in the sixties. Even today it's immediately obvious why they, and the show, created such a huge impact at the time. They still have an innocent fun about them, combined with amazing glamour. They took their work seriously, but they also lived the life and partied like no one before them. As the sixties became the seventies, Pan's People, like *Top of the Pops* itself, went on to even greater heights, and a new, even more spectacular age began.

Above: Pan's People in their colour-coded outfits – like the Spice Girls, they each had their own trademark costume colours when the show moved from black-and-white to colour.

MICK JAGGER caught in relaxed mood backstage at *Top of the Pops*. The Stones were on the very first edition of the show, and were regulars throughout the sixties.

KEITH RICHARDS looking young and fresh-faced at *Top of the Pops* in Manchester. The band made seven appearances during the Manchester years.

CLIFF RICHARD had been in the business for six years by the time *Top of the Pops* was launched. He went on to gain the record for the most appearances on the show.

DIANA ROSS, seen here at the show on 7 October 1964, when she sang 'Baby Love' with The Supremes. The performance is one of the few to have survived from the early years.

JIMI HENDRIX photographed at BBC Television Centre on 18 January 1967, about to record his only ever appearance on *Top of the Pops*.

CHER — hippie outfits had never been seen before on *Top of the Pops* when Cher arrived at the BBC in Manchester in August 1965 to perform 'I Got You Babe' with her partner Sonny Bono.

JULIE DRISCOLL shows off the classic sixties look for her performance of 'This Wheel's On Fire' with Brian Auger and the Trinity in April 1968. It was their only hit, but was later re-recorded as the theme for the BBC television programme *Absolutely Fabulous*.

STEVIE WONDER was still 'Little' Stevie Wonder when he appeared aged 15 on *Top of the Pops* of 20 January 1966 with his first hit, 'Uptight'.

TOM JONES still manages to look cool over a cup of tea in his dressing room at *Top of the Pops*. His debut was on 11 February 1965 with 'It's Not Unusual'.

TINA TURNER, seen here on 23 June 1966, preparing to sing 'River Deep, Mountain High' with husband Ike. They were paid the unprecedented fee of £700 for their performance, as was Percy Sledge, who appeared on the same programme.

1970s

If the sixties were a golden era for *Top of the Pops*, then the seventies were an age when the show glittered. The programme was now in colour, but the mood of the show was different as well. Britain in the seventies was not a joyous place: the economy was in trouble, there were power cuts and the three-day week, and the country was beleaguered by constant strikes. It was in these troubled times that the *Top of the Pops* audience was at its height, watching a parade of superstars like Marc Bolan, David Bowie, Rod Stewart, Elton John and Queen. *Top of the Pops* became an escape from the viewers' dreary lives, with its bizarre men in make-up, beautiful girls in hot pants, and stars who glittered on the screen like Christmas decorations. As the decade moved on, dressing up became the norm, and Glam Rock was born. Band after band tried to outdo each other with increasingly wild and outrageous costumes and make-up, and the audience loved it.

Icons of the seventies: Abba, David Bowie, Marc Bolan (opposite, left to right) and Freddie Mercury and Queen (below).

Above: Yoko Ono and John Lennon at *Top of the Pops* on 5 February 1970, to perform 'Instant Karma' with The Plastic Ono Band. Yoko wore a blindfold for the recording, while John had an armband bearing the slogan 'People For Peace'.

The lost archive

Before looking at *Top of the Pops*' seventies heyday, first we should acknowledge a tragedy. The move to colour was a massive change for the BBC, and gave *Top of the Pops* a huge boost that kept viewers mesmerized. But the changeover was also a big upheaval for the Corporation as a whole – new cameras and equipment, new forms of lighting and costume. Suddenly, colour was the new thing, and black and white was passé, a format confined to the dustbin of history. So what possible use could the hours and hours of black-and-white archive be, now that all programmes were in colour? Tape had always been expensive, so weekly shows like *Top of the Pops* were encouraged to recycle. After all, what interest would pop music hold for future generations? Thousands of classic performances were lost in this way.

Nothing now exists of appearances by Jimi Hendrix, Aretha Franklin, Fleetwood Mac, The Beach Boys, Dusty Springfield or The Monkees. The Beatles' 'Paperback Writer' and 'Rain' were also wiped. Only a few black-and-white episodes escaped the purge. From the Dickenson Road era only a handful of performances remain, by The Stones, The Supremes, Sonny and Cher and The Byrds. It's been said that *Top of the Pops* survived *despite* the BBC, and the destruction of the archive provides no better evidence. The producer of the time, Stan Dorfman, says despairingly, 'The BBC constantly treated us like the dirty end of something. The bosses didn't understand the show at all. They felt we were necessary, but that we should be pushed aside, because it wasn't what the BBC should be doing.'

Seventies stars

Stan's word 'necessary' refers to the audience figures. The BBC couldn't axe *Top of the Pops* because it pulled in such huge numbers, around 20 million a week. *Top of the Pops* was, by now, essential family viewing: it went out on a Thursday night, and everyone talked about it the next day. Kids would watch the rundown from Twenty to One, picking out their favourites, dads would say that 'it wasn't like their day', and mums would love it when Cliff was on. Everyone wanted to be in the audience and there was rumoured to be a four-year waiting list. The kids in the audience just seemed so cool, dancing along to the tunes, and waving to their mums. Well, anyone would look cool standing next to Jimmy Savile.

Viewers were rewarded with a parade of superstars during the early seventies – none greater than John Lennon, who appeared on 5 February 1970. The Beatles still hadn't officially split up, but it was clear there were chronic differences within the group and they were all going their separate ways. John released 'Instant Karma', and he and Yoko made a film to go with the tune, which they were very proud of. It featured the two of them flying around in a giant white balloon. John personally called the producer of *Top of the Pops* to ask him to show it. Yes, of course, came the answer – if you'll come in and play it live as well.

Apple's Tony Bramwell was plugging the record. 'We instantly got some guys together who could be The Plastic Ono Band – Klaus Voorman, Alan White on drums, [Beatles road manager] Mal Evans playing tambourine, I think there was an Irish journalist on guitar.' And, of course, Yoko Ono. It was a crucial performance for John, and he was terribly nervous. People who were there say it was very strange to see perhaps the most famous man in the world sitting patiently outside the studio with his sheet music, waiting to go on and perform, as if he was sitting in a doctor's waiting room. It was very strange, too, for Yoko – she was widely blamed for the break-up of The Beatles, and people didn't know how to treat her. But, being Yoko, she had a trick up her sleeve. The idea was that, during the number, she would sit on a stool holding up signs that read 'Peace', 'Love', etc. Fine. When it came to the take, she came on blindfolded. As the number began, the PA in the gallery pointed out that the blindfold was actually a sanitary towel. Needless to say, there were no close-ups of Yoko and her signs. 'It was art,' says Bramwell. 'Yoko was art. But it was one of John's best rock 'n' roll performances 'cos he did a live vocal on it, which was excellent. A really important moment.'

As the decade rolled on, more and more stars appeared. In September 1971, there was the famous performance of 'Maggie May' by Rod Stewart, in which Rod kicks a football around with Ronnie Wood, while his mate John Peel mimes a mandolin solo. The same year, Marc Bolan appeared with 'Get It On', complete with pink trousers, silver jacket, stars painted on his face – and Elton John on piano. In 1972, it was David Bowie with 'Starman', in a multicoloured bodysuit, with Mick Ronson in a gold, zip-up catsuit. These exotic birds of paradise, with long hair and make-up, may have seemed threatening to many. Such sights had never appeared on TV before: when Bowie put his arm round Ronson during 'Starman', a million dads around the country probably recoiled in horror at the sight of two men actually embracing. You have only to look at the ordinariness of the studio audience at that time – the lads in tank tops and brown trousers and the girls in roll-neck jumpers and pleated skirts – to understand why stars like Bowie and Bolan shocked and shone on *Top of the Pops*. But there was more to come: the scene was set for Glam Rock.

Glam Rock was the first and last musical genre that was solely created on and because of *Top of the Pops*. If the show hadn't existed, there would have been no Glam Rock.

Right: Slade had 18 hits and 6 Number Ones during the seventies.

Above: Ushering in the Glam Rock era, David Bowie caused shock and horror as he embraced Mick Ronson during his June 1972 performance of 'Starman'.
Opposite: The Bay City Rollers were forced to film their performances in secret after the BBC banned them from live shows when their fans besieged TV Centre.

Glam Rock was the first and last musical genre that was solely created on and because of *Top of the Pops*. If the show hadn't existed, there would have been no Glam Rock. Bolan and Bowie had opened the door – now acts like Slade, Wizzard, Gary Glitter and Sweet took up the mantle and covered it in glitter. Week after week, bands tried to outdo each other, to be more spectacular and out-rageous. Costumes were specially made, even guitars were designed just for *Top of the Pops* appearances. Roy Wood and Wizzard went in for face make-up and masses of hair, Gary Glitter's outfits lived up to his name as he strutted and pouted his singalong tunes, and Sweet sported platforms, more glitter, and a strangely androgynous bass player. 'Roy Wood used to look at what Sweet were doing and go back to the dressing room and quickly change his act,' says one record-company promotions man. 'He'd always try to outdo them. Let's get the bass player on skates!' But kings of them all were Slade, thanks not just to Noddy Holder's famous mirrored hats, but also the antics of guitarist Dave Hill, who spared no effort – even shaving his head on one occasion – to enter-tain the audience.

Teen idols

As if the regular parade of superstars and glam rockers wasn't enough, *Top of the Pops* in the early seventies was also invaded by a new form of mayhem: the teen idols. Ten years earlier, Beatlemania had prevented the Fab Four from appearing on the show. Now, the scenes of teenage hysteria were repeated for The Osmonds, David Cassidy and, of course, The Bay City Rollers. First up, though, were The Jackson 5. They debuted on *Top of the Pops* in 1972 with 'Rockin' Robin'. Soon, however, The Jackson 5 found themselves rivals to another clean-cut bunch of brothers, The Osmonds.

Tony Bramwell had seen it all before. By this time, he was head of promotions at Polydor and knew how to choreograph the hysteria. 'With the Osmonds and the Jackson 5,' he says, 'it was like an ongoing battle between the two record companies as to who could stir up the biggest fanmania. It was between Donny and Little Jimmy, and young Michael. One time, they were both in hotels on opposite sides of Grosvenor Square. They were just causing havoc. We'd deliberately stir up fan controversy. It was never a secret that The Osmonds would be at Television Centre

▶▶ Noddy Holder

Noddy and Slade became *Top of the Pops'* house band in the Glam Rock era.

I used to watch *Top of the Pops* from day one. Obviously, I was a music fan in my youth — I started making music when I was seven years old. I used to flip out when *Top of the Pops* had The Beatles, The Who, The Kinks on. And I used to love all the black acts they had on, all the Motown acts. I remember it was a ritual, the whole family gathered round the TV to watch *Top of the Pops*. Even if your dad used to slag off the acts that were on, it was still a family thing. It was a mixed bag in those days in the charts. You could have The Beatles or The Who on alongside Ken Dodd or Engelbert or Des O'Connor. Something for all the family.

We made our first appearance in 1970 and our last appearance in 1991, so we had 21 years on *Top of the Pops*. Apart from the times when we were Number One, and had to close the show, we were always first act on. Every producer and director always liked us to open the show, because we were a raucous band and they knew they'd get a good atmosphere going with the studio audience. They used to call us the House Band from about '71 to '75. We had 18 chart records during the seventies — remember that records used to stick around for weeks in the charts, so for each record, we might have gone on five or six times. And it stood us in good stead.

It was a very colourful time, the Glam Rock era. It was a time when anything went, really. Spearheaded by ourselves and Marc Bolan, we made music a lot more colourful. We knew that we had to go on TV and actually shock people. Love us or hate us, as long as people were talking about us in the pubs the next day, that's all we needed to do. So we started off with low-key outfits, but then as the Glam Rock era kicked in,

everybody else dressed more and more outrageously, and we had to go one better. About 1974, 1975, it all got out of hand, with all the bands like Sweet and Gary Glitter all trying to outdo each other. But in our band, Dave Hill wasn't having any of it, he would not let anybody outdo him. He wanted to be more and more outrageous every time he appeared. He used to go in the toilet to get dressed, so we never saw his outfits until he'd got the whole regalia on. We used to say, 'come out Dave. R-r-r-reveal all.' He'd come out, and we'd all fall about on the floor pissing ourselves laughing at whatever he'd got on. His favourite saying was, 'You write 'em, I'll sell 'em'.

He had some amazing outfits. There was one that was all covered in feathers. The nickname for that was Foghorn Leghorn, after the cartoon chicken. There was one that was like a Cleopatra wig, but made of metal, which we used to call the Metal Nun. It was ridiculous, because he could never move about in them, they were all so heavy. Visually though, it all made *Top of the Pops* very exciting in that period. Superb.

In the early seventies, in the Glam Rock period, things socially and economically were very poor. There were a lot of power cuts, the miners were on strike, there were loads of strikes. And in those sort of times, people turn to showbiz, they want to be taken into fantasy land. I think the Glam Rock era got people out of their everyday lives. The music was very uplifting, very fun. It was the days when people used to tune into *Top of the Pops* specifically to see what antics a band like us was getting up to, what we were wearing, what was the gimmick that particular week. It was good for us, and good for the show.

Below, left: Michael Jackson appeared with his brothers on the Christmas show in 1972 for 'Rockin' Robin'.
Below, right: More sibling success, Donny and Marie Osmond appeared on the show in January 1979.

or the Jackson 5 would be there. It would be announced to their fans, to cause as much chaos as you could in W12 [the postcode of TV Centre]. It was very similar to when the Beatles used to turn up anywhere. Even very young girls just going berserk. It was just thousands of them – all dressed as Osmonds or whatever – creating general mayhem in Wood Lane.'

Not to be outdone, the Brits came up with their own version – or, rather, the Scots did. From 1974 onwards, The Bay City Rollers caused more hysteria than the Osmonds and the Jackson 5 put together. When The Rollers first appeared on *Top of the Pops*, Television

Centre was besieged, with all five entrances blocked by teenage girls. 'Not only could nobody get in,' says Jimmy Savile, 'nobody could get out either. There were people from all these great programmes, current affairs shows like *Panorama*, and they couldn't get out of Television Centre for screaming dervishes at every single gate.' Enough was enough. It was one thing suffering *Top of the Pops* every week, but to have News and Current Affairs disrupted by pop stars was beyond the limit. An edict was issued from on high that no group or artist with a young teenage following would be allowed to

Left: Marc Bolan displays typical showmanship as he poses with his band backstage at *Top of the Pops*. Shots like these were used to illustrate the weekly chart rundown.

perform at Television Centre. For David Cassidy, that meant missing out on *Top of the Pops*. 'I was never allowed to perform on *Top of the Pops*,' he says. 'I was told there'd be too many security problems.'

Typically, the BBC had once more missed the point of *Top of the Pops*, by banning the very people that youngsters were most interested in, but the show managed to get round it. For Cassidy's 'Daydreamer', a film was made showing him arriving at Heathrow. The later Bay City Rollers performances were shot in secret without an audience, although to make up for it sometimes viewers got a little extra; for example, 'Give A Little Love' was filmed with the lads perched on the bonnets of four Rolls Royces, lined up in a row. Yes, the Rollers ... on Rollers! They don't make television like that any more.

In 1975, another superstar appeared from the other end of the rock 'n' roll spectrum. Throughout its first ten years *Top of the Pops* had always featured the crooners who crept into the charts occasionally – Matt Monro, Ken Dodd, Des O'Connor. But to have the daddy of them all, Bing Crosby, appearing on the show was something very special. He was an old-school Hollywood star who happened to have sold 30 million copies of just one single, 'White Christmas'. And on 24 July 1975, he arrived to perform his new one, 'That's What Life Is All About'. One junior record-company promoter who was in the studio that day was a young lad called Pete Waterman. 'I walked in and there

was Bing Crosby,' he says. 'I couldn't quite believe it. You went to *Top of the Pops* and there was always somebody massive there every week, and you never took it too seriously. But there was Bing Crosby. You were in the presence of somebody that was bigger than anybody else could ever be.'

Bing was a true gent all day: people were taken into his dressing room to meet him, and afterwards he hosted a huge dinner for the crew. But the producer of that show, Robin Nash, also remembers that old Bing was very distracted in the studio. 'He was very interested in Pan's People,' he says. 'After his rehearsal, we couldn't get him back to his dressing room.' There were more distractions to come. The former prime minister, Edward Heath, was a lifelong fan of Crosby and happened to be in TV Centre for an interview with Robin Day. 'I was directing that programme myself,' says Nash, 'and I suddenly looked up and thought, "I know that face." I realized it was Edward Heath.' Musical director Johnny Pearson also got a shock. 'I felt a tap on my shoulder, and it was the former prime minister saying, "Do you think you could get Bing Crosby's autograph for me?"' But, despite the presence of an ex-prime minister in the studio, the star remained focused. In fact, if you watch the recording, you'll see that Bing's last words are, 'Go girls, go,' as he looks longingly across the studio at the lovely Pan's People preparing for their number.

'Flick Colby and I used to discuss that we probably needed to do a "gymslip" number every so often because that intrigued a certain audience.'

PRODUCER ROBIN NASH

Above: Legs & Co got their name through a viewers' competition – (top to bottom) Lulu Cartwright, Rosie Hetherington, Patti Hammond, Pauline Peters, Gill Clark and Sue Menhennick.

Pan's become Legs

By 1976, Pan's People had been going for eight years. They were still huge stars on the show, but eight years is a long time in the life of a dancer, especially when you're working every single week. Andi had left in 1972 to have a baby, and was replaced by the much younger Cherry Gillespie (Cherry was 'unveiled' to the other girls when she popped out of a giant Christmas present, before joining them to dance around to Nilsson's 'Without You' in a big white nightdress). But Ruth, Dee Dee, Babs and Louise had been there since the sixties – getting paid Equity minimum every week – and each of them wanted to go their own way. 'What happens with dancers is that they get old,' says Flick Colby. 'Not all at the same time,

but each girl individually decided she'd had enough for one reason or another. Illness, injury, marriage, whatever. And the camera's cruel. They certainly felt that they had had enough of *Top of the Pops*.'

Flick was also aware that the music was changing. She'd always been conscious of what was going on in the clubs, and she spotted the early signs of disco. She knew that a group of showgirls parading around was limiting and dated. Pan's had always been their own managers, and controlled what they did, so one day in April 1976 they just stopped. Without telling their bosses, they danced their last number to the Four Seasons' 'Silver Star' and when the news leaked out after the programme, there was massive press coverage, national mourning – and a very angry Bill Cotton (now running BBC1), who was furious that he hadn't been consulted.

Flick had lined up a replacement group, whom she managed alongside Pan's Ruth Pearson. The name of the group, Ruby Flipper, was made up of the letters of Flick Colby and Ruth P's names (well, nearly), and there was to be a big innovation – the new *Top of the Pops* dance group would have men in it. 'Ruby Flipper was kinda kooky,' says Flick. 'It was three women and two men. I wanted to have a group of dancers to reflect the music more, and sometimes you need men. Sometimes it isn't a women's kind of song, so I had men in the group. But for some reason it didn't work. I don't know why.'

Well, one reason is clear: there was a not-so-subtle campaign against Ruby Flipper. One of the guys, Floyd, was black, and in times that were very different from today, there were suggestions that the public didn't want to see a black man dancing suggestively with a white woman. Those suggestions came from within the BBC.

Quite aside from this, Bill Cotton's nose was severely out of joint. He'd invented *Top of the Pops*, and knew the value of having an all-girl group. 'Flick and I were summoned up to his office,' says Ruth. 'We tried to look as innocent as possible. But he said he didn't like the concept and that he wanted a girl group back on the show. We tried to explain to him that the time had gone for girl groups and the show needed something different. It was tired. Things out there were changing. But basically he told us you either form another girl group, or you lose the gig. He had us by the short and curlies.'

'I was told to re-form an all-girl group – or quit,' echoes Flick. 'It was as simple as that.'

After just six months, Ruby Flipper danced their last number on 14 October 1976, to a track that was ironic, to say the least: 'Play That Funky Music, White Boy' by Wild Cherry. Flick managed to get Floyd a job – on *The Black and White Minstrel Show*, where he was obliged to put black make-up over his black skin so he didn't stand out from the other minstrels.

The public were asked to choose the name for the new all-girl group, after they made their debut dancing to the theme from *Jaws*. The opening shot was from underwater, with the girls' legs dangling down, so the name Legs & Co wasn't a great surprise. The three girls from Ruby Flipper – Sue, Patti and Lulu – were all members, along with new girls Pauline, fresh from the West End stage, 17-year-old Rosie and beauty-queen Gill, a finalist in the Miss UK competition. She told Flick she'd take the job only if she didn't win the contest. Thankfully, Gill came second.

Flick and Ruth admit that they were just doing a job with Legs & Co. The girls were all very good dancers, all very attractive and hard-working, but they were a manufactured group. 'They didn't have the hunger, they hadn't known the lean times that Pan's People had known,' says Ruth. 'They didn't party the way we used to party. Flick and I were always amazed at how well behaved they all were.'

Nevertheless, they were a huge hit with the public, and it worked for the show. The people soon had their favourites, and Legs & Co did the job of providing the glamour. Producer Robin Nash admits, 'We still had the dads watching. They wanted to see a pretty leg occasionally and Legs & Co were that. I'll be quite honest that Flick Colby and I used to discuss that we probably needed to do a "gymslip" number every so often because that intrigued a certain audience.'

The way Legs & Co worked was a double-edged sword for Flick. Her creative ambitions were inevitably stifled by the BBC manage-

Above, left: Ruby Flipper's Patti and Floyd caused controversy within the BBC with their routines, and the group was axed after six months.
Above, right: Legs & Co 'flowered up' for their version of 'Mah Na Mah Na'. The sixth 'leg', Sue, was dressed as a bumble bee.

Right: When The Sex Pistols were banned from the show, *Top of the Pops* dressed Legs & Co in 'punk' outfits to dance to their songs.

ment. She wasn't allowed to develop the act or explore new avenues, although she was given more money to spend on the routines. The costumes became more lavish and each week a new set would be built – ballrooms, desert islands, rooftops, pools and street scenes – all for the girls to show off their talents. 'It could go from the sublime to the ridiculous,' says Legs & Co member Sue. 'One week you could be wearing the sequins, the fake furs, the diamonds. The next week, you could be dressed as a Smurf, or running around with a loaf of French bread in your hand. I never understood that then and I still don't understand it now.'

There was also the famous literal choreography: 'Daddy Was A Bank Robber' featured the girls behind bars, carrying bags marked 'Swag'; 'I Can't Stand the Rain' showed each of them in a see-through plastic mac with a bikini underneath, splashing around in red wellies in real water. Yes, these were the days when you could turn the sound down on *Top of the Pops*, and still know which number Legs & Co were dancing to.

As the seventies went on, though, Legs & Co came in for some stick from feminists. The phrase 'political correctness' came into the vocabulary, and it was clear that Legs & Co – parading round in their bikinis every week – were far from politically correct. Promotions man Richard Evans couldn't believe the

routine they came up with for a song he was plugging called 'Typically Tropical'. 'The dance routine is absolutely classic,' he says. 'It was air hostesses stripping. Absolute cliché. They started out as fully dressed, uniformed stewardesses and finished off in bikinis. Talk about lack of political correctness – it could only have been worse if it'd been nurses.'

Flick is quick to defend her work. 'I've always had trouble with feminists,' she says, 'but I've never felt like a second-class citizen, and I certainly never made any of my dancers feel like second-class citizens. I think people did see the girls as objects, but I don't think that was fair, because people knew our names and we were in control of our own lives. We ran our own group, we did the business side and nobody ever made us do anything we didn't want to do.'

'A lot of it was tongue in cheek anyway, not to be taken too seriously,' adds another Leg, Lulu. 'We were all trained dancers, so we probably sold our souls compared to the classical people, but it was a career. We thought of it as more than a bit of totty.'

Most of the sexism of the time was innocent enough. But there was a dark side as well. It wasn't unusual in the seventies for the crew to pick out the prettiest girls from the audience, and ask them to stay behind after the show and dance for them – under the pretext

of testing some new cameras. There was worse going on in the dressing rooms, which almost led the show into deep trouble. 'We had to be very careful, because there were scandals,' says a source who was working on the show in the early seventies. 'We were aware that there were girls who might have been below age being taken into dressing rooms by artists. Guys would be caught with girls in their dressing rooms. The girls in the audience would do anything to get to their idols.' Word reached Scotland Yard, and they took the matter seriously enough to investigate. 'We had police in our offices. There was a red-headed cop, who interviewed us and stayed with us through the whole production. Apparently, there had been complaints about kids being screwed in the dressing rooms. He was there for a week in the office. But nothing hit the fan.'

Punk

By the late seventies, music was changing. 'Punk rock? I tried to block it out of my mind,' says Tony Blackburn, who was still presenting in 1977, after 10 years as host. 'I hated punk and the punk era. It was horrible.' Blackburn wasn't alone in his contempt for the music on the programme.

Different people have different memories of how *Top of the Pops* dealt – or, rather, failed to deal – with punk. Looking back, some fans

insist that most of the punk bands were either banned or unwilling to go on an 'establishment' show. Yet in 1977, The Jam and The Stranglers made their debut and the following year, The Buzzcocks, Sham 69, The Boomtown Rats, X-Ray Specs, and Ian Dury and the Blockheads all arrived. One name is conspicuous by its absence – The Sex Pistols. Their promoter claims that they wanted to appear, but their biggest hit of that year, 'God Save the Queen', was judged to be inappropriate at the time of Her Majesty's Silver Jubilee, and was instantly banned.

Like it or not, *Top of the Pops* relied on the chart and when punk bands entered the charts they couldn't be ignored. It was a meeting of opposites: *Top of the Pops*, still an old-school BBC Light Entertainment show at heart, run by upper-class, middle-aged men; and the punks, young, uncouth rebels, hating everything – or, at least, pretending to. 'There was always a tension in the studio when a punk band appeared,' says one promoter. 'The BBC used to think, "Oh no, punk! Nastiness!" But these kids used to behave really well. They knew they had to do it to sell records.'

Cliff Richard was still appearing regularly on *Top of the Pops* at the time. 'We're led to believe that all punk bands were wild bullies who spat on people,' he says. 'But I was always amazed that you'd meet people who were

'ABBA were the most professional band I've ever worked with,' he says. 'But they did like a drink. In Sweden, Scotch and Champagne are very expensive. So when they came over the girls liked a little tipple.'

JUDD LANDER

Above, left: ABBA performing 'Fernando' on the show in April 1976. Above, right: Boney M at a full dress rehearsal for the show.

actually fairly ordinary and that a lot of it was an act.' Sham 69, for example, polished their act well. Jimmy Pursey would fall over on the floor, precisely on cue, for each of the endless rehearsals so that the camera could catch his great 'moment' when it came to the take.

But the real issue wasn't whether the punks were acting or not, or even whether *Top of the Pops* successfully reflected the punk hits. The punk acts who appeared on the show were in the charts, and therefore they had in some way bought into the Top 40 game. Real punk, though, was happening in clubs and on the street – a million miles away from *Top of the Pops* – and it was changing attitudes to music. The music that 'the kids' were into was further from the mainstream than ever before, and that was what *Top of the Pops* ignored. A new

generation felt that they didn't own *Top of the Pops*, and it just wasn't for them. Comedian Sean Hughes was one of the disenfranchised. 'I went out and bought "God Save the Queen", and it was banned from the radio and TV,' he says. 'I watched *Top of the Pops* that week and they said, the highest new entry is "God Save the Queen" by The Sex Pistols, but we can't play it. I thought yeah, *Top of the Pops* are chicken.'

Top of the Pops still looked the same, with the same presenters, the same glittery set, still blithely trying to entertain a family audience and to reflect all tastes. The running orders became simply bizarre. On 20 September 1978 The Buzzcocks, The Skids and The Jam were on the same show as Brotherhood of Man, Leo Sayer and The Three Degrees, with a bit of ABBA and 10CC thrown in for good measure. Instead of something for everyone, there was something to alienate everyone.

Pluggers

Meanwhile, the internal workings of the show had got out of hand. The late seventies were still a time of massive singles sales for the likes of Boney M, ABBA, The Bee Gees and Blondie – and *Top of the Pops* had a huge, if maturing, audience. Record companies were making money like there was no tomorrow and *Top of the Pops* was still their main shop window. By now, the strange breed of sales-man known as 'the plugger' had evolved into a sophisticated being. There were around a dozen men with unlimited expense accounts,

▸▸ Eric Hall

'Monster monster' Eric Hall was a legendary plugger for EMI records.

In those days when I was the monster monster plugger, I was the best ever TV promotion man in the country. I was the Maradona of Music, the Pele of Pop. There weren't that many pop shows, and you knew when you got *Top of the Pops*, your record would go 'zoom' to the top of the chart. One *Top of the Pops* was worth maybe 500 radio plays. Forget Radio 1, Radio 2 . . . give me one *Top of the Pops*, that's good enough for me.

I plugged everyone from Frank Sinatra to the Sex Pistols, but the biggest star I plugged was Marc Bolan. He was, like me, an egomaniac, and he loved to camp it up, like the old saying that when you opened the fridge door, he'd do 20 minutes. He loved the dressing up, he loved the visuals, just to be different . . . bright colours and jackets and things. He loved performing, he loved an audience. He had charisma, and you just can't buy that. There might only be a hundred people in front of him at *Top of the Pops*, but he knew that that massive TV audience was out there, and he loved it.

One day, at the Tuesday morning meetings they used to have, someone couldn't do the show because their work permit hadn't come through. So Robin Nash [the producer] went for the next in the chart, which was Queen doing 'Seven Seas of Rye'. That gave Queen their first break. Freddie Mercury was such a great showman, but he hated doing *Top of the Pops*. I used to say to him, 'Freddie, we're doing *Top of the Pops* on Wednesday.'

'Oh, do we have to, my dear?' Freddie didn't really like doing it because you had to play all these games because of the Musicians' Union rules that said you had to go in and re-record your backing track. But there was no way you could go and do

'Killer Queen' again for *Top of the Pops* in three hours, when it took about six months to record it. That's why after a little time we started going into the video thing and made all these wonderful videos.

When I first heard 'Bohemian Rhapsody', I hated it, to be honest. When Freddie first played it to me, I thought he was taking the mickey. He put it on and it was all this about killing a man and putting a gun to his head. It's hardly a toe-tapper, is it? You know, you want a toe-tapper. So I said, 'Freddie, when is it going to get a bit more fast?' so he says, 'Listen, my dear, listen.' So it goes, 'Mama, da da da.' Stop. So I thought, it's over now, and I went to take the tape off. Then suddenly, it went 'Scaramoosh,' whoosh, and it started all over again. I had to tell him it was too, too long. Originally it was about 16 minutes long. We cut back about four or five minutes out of it. But it was still too long for *Top of the Pops*, so they didn't actually use it until it got to Number One.

The BBC bar on the fourth floor was a plugging environment, really. If you had an act on, you were in the bar to try and get someone on for next week. If you didn't have an act on, you'd be there anyway because you'd know that all the main people all went to the bar after the show. So you plugged them. Got them drunk and plugged them. I used to get champagne for everybody. Champagne, champagne. I used to spend a fortune on my drinks bill. Well, EMI's drinks bill. One time, Cliff Richard stood up in the bar, and announced, 'Eric Hall's expenses have just gone platinum.' It was wonderful, loved it. I miss it. I do miss *Top of the Pops*.

whose job was simply to get certain records played on *Top of the Pops*. Many of their efforts, of course, were a waste of time, because the programme was based on the chart, which was chosen by the public, not the producers. Nevertheless, they could have fun going through the motions of plugging their records. And, boy, did they have fun.

At the end of the seventies, men like Tony Bramwell, Eric Hall, Richard Evans, Paddy Flemming and Judd Lander lived the most exciting lives any of us could ever imagine, hanging around with superstar pop acts, surrounded by all the trappings of the showbiz lifestyle, and spending thousands and thousands of pounds of record-company money entertaining the *Top of the Pops* crew.

'We used to spend our evenings taking television people out for dinners and payola-ing them,' says Tony Bramwell. 'We just used to take them out and entertain them together with the girls from Pan's People or Legs & Co, who always came along as a side cabaret. We had tables in all the best restaurants. It was very cosy.'

Cosy indeed, as the pluggers almost became part of the crew. Getting into Television Centre was easy. For years, the commissionaires thought Judd Lander was actually Bill Cotton's son, and used to wave him through like he was royalty. Others got into the building claiming to be heating engineers or maintenance men in order to present themselves at the *Top of the Pops* offices. For

most of them, it was all fun and games. On one occasion, a group of pluggers even found their way onto the screen, dancing behind The Wurzels, wearing T-shirts for a fictional association called the 'British Union of Record Pluggers' – or 'BURP'. Printed on their backs was 'First Annual Regional Tour', or 'FART'.

The pluggers would try any stunt to draw attention to their records. One guy had himself delivered in a crate to the producer's office. Others camped out in the office – literally camped in a tent – overnight to surprise the crew in the morning. But the main tool of plugging was alcohol.

'I'm sure it didn't influence their decisions in any way at all,' says Richard Evans, who plugged Thin Lizzy, 10CC, Tom Jones and Shakin' Stevens. Innocently, he insists, 'The great thing about *Top of the Pops* is that we couldn't really influence their decision,

because you only got on if you were in the chart. But there was a little grey area, because there used to be five "breakers", so if you worked it really well, you could sometimes get in there. And two or three times a year, it'd give your record company a great big hit.'

Producer Robin Nash insists, 'They never used to go beyond inviting one out for a meal, buying a drink after the show. They did learn very quickly there was no possibility of influence, because the programme made itself, based on the rules.' But another senior figure of the time says there was more to it. 'Radio 1 had been done for payola,' he points out. 'That was a scare that affected *Top of the Pops*. We were hugely susceptible to payola, for slots like "Tip for the Top", which was the producer's choice. I must admit there were pluggers that one had friendships with, and I suppose one would tend to favour their

Far left: Elton John's first appearance on *Top of the Pops* was as a backing singer for Brotherhood of Man, but he went on to have a string of massive solo hits.
Left: Roger Daltrey and The Who in full flight on the 500th edition of *Top of the Pops*.

artists.' Citing the kind of pressure the team came under, he says, 'In the clubs, they would literally pour alcohol down your throat. And offers of anything, literally anything, to play the records. At Christmas, all kinds of things would turn up. You might keep a bottle of Scotch, but golf clubs, anything would arrive at the house and you had to send them back.'

The BBC was clearly uncomfortable with what *Top of the Pops* had become. On screen, it was looking dated and out of touch with the young audience it was supposed to serve. Behind the scenes, while never actually corrupt, it was felt by some to be a little too cosy with the record companies. It was time for a new regime and, in 1980, there arrived a new broom with very hard bristles. Within 12 months, Michael Hurll had made *Top of the Pops* an utterly different show – and its glory days were well and truly over.

The Who's performance on the 500th edition of *Top of the Pops* ended with Keith Moon and Pete Townsend both smashing their instruments — but producers felt it was too violent for family viewing, and edited the instrument-smashing out of the final show. The Who's unpredictable behaviour resulted in them being banned from the programme for a number of years.

JOHN LENNON at *Top of the Pops* on 5 February 1970 to perform 'Instant Karma'. The Beatles hadn't officially split up, but Lennon was already on his third solo single, joined on the show by Yoko and The Plastic Ono Band.

GEORGE HARRISON turned up at *Top of the Pops* not as a performer, but as a producer of two hits by the Radha Krishna Temple. He refused to appear on stage, but stood behind the camera directing the performance by the Krishna devotees.

MICHAEL JACKSON, aged 14, at the Christmas show of 1972. It was the year Michael became established as a solo artist, and was also the last time he appeared in person on the show.

ELTON JOHN — despite a huge run of hits, Elton only appeared five times on the show during the seventies, three times in his own right, once with Marc Bolan, and once as presenter.

BRIAN FERRY — Roxy Music had started as a Glam Rock band, but by the time of their biggest hits, Brian Ferry was a tuxedo-clad smoothie on *Top of the Pops*.

KATE BUSH making her debut on *Top of the Pops* in February 1978 with 'Wuthering Heights'. As the seventies went on, like many acts, she preferred to promote her work through video.

MARC BOLAN made five appearances between 1971 and 1977, either solo or with T Rex. His first was for 'Get It On', when the band were joined by Elton John on piano.

ROD STEWART appeared five times on *Top of the Pops* in the early 70s, including twice with The Faces. The most memorable was for 'Maggie May', with John Peel playing mandolin, and Ronnie Wood kicking a football around during the instrumental break.

60

ABBA, caught backstage at *Top of the Pops* the day after they won the Eurovision Song Contest with 'Waterloo'.

DEBBIE HARRY of Blondie making her debut on the show with 'Denis' in February 1978.

1980s

Things were different in the eighties, and so was *Top of the Pops*. In 1980 a new producer, Michael Hurll, came on board, with a vision that was strikingly different from what had gone before. After sticking to virtually the same look throughout the seventies, suddenly in 1980, the show looked different — and noticeably echoed the mood of the times. DJ Janice Long was

Above: Grace Jones.
Opposite, top: Morrissey.
Opposite, bottom left: Young Guns George Michael and Andrew Ridgley in Wham!
Opposite, bottom right: Gary Numan.

one of the presenters who backcombed her hair, and put on lipgloss and huge earrings. 'It was Thatcher's Britain,' she says. 'There was money. People showed off the fact that they had money. And *Top of the Pops* represented what was going on politically. It was *Dynasty* and *Dallas*, wasn't it? It was a greedy time, and a terribly ostentatious time — no point in being subtle.' Of course, some great bands came along in the eighties — Spandau, Duran, Wham!, Frankie, The Smiths — but it was almost as if *Top of the Pops* wasn't about the music: it was about the atmosphere, the excitement and the spirit of the times.

Above: By the eighties, the all-girl dance groups had been replaced by a mixed troupe of dancers and wannabes known as 'Zoo'.

Thatcher's Britain

In Thatcher's 'can do' Britain, nothing was impossible. New producer Michael Hurll put the audience in full view, and it seemed anyone who wanted to get on the show could do so simply by dressing outrageously and dancing enthusiastically. As the decade went on, this spirit infused the music as well – anyone with a synthesizer could knock off a tune in their back bedroom and end up on *Top of the Pops*. And a new bunch of wannabes even got to present the show – the Radio 1 jocks were controversially swept away and replaced by a group of kids who'd barely taken their first steps on the TV ladder.

Throughout the eighties, *Top of the Pops* seemed like a non-stop party, but there's no doubt that the programme suffered. Look back on the footage, and it all seems terribly dated and fake, with its cheerleaders, over-enthusiastic presenters (sorry Anthea) and a parade of faceless dance acts miming badly to their one-hit wonders. Meanwhile, television itself was changing, another direct effect of the spirit of competition under Thatcher. Channel 4, MTV, even the BBC's own 'yoof' programmes all nibbled away at *Top of the Pops*' monopoly, and made viewers question the show. In tune with the times? Maybe, maybe not. But by the end of the eighties, *Top of the Pops* was in a bad way.

A new broom

'When I took over *Top of the Pops*, I was going to make some changes,' says Michael Hurll ominously. 'We made it more like a party.' That simple word, 'party', set the tone for what *Top of the Pops* became when Hurll joined in 1980.

There's no doubt that the way *Top of the Pops* was being run in the late seventies had got out of hand, and the show definitely needed to be taken under control. 'It was falling to bits,' says choreographer Flick Colby, who'd been there since 1968 and had seen various regimes come and go. 'It needed a firm hand – and he certainly had a firm hand.' DJ John Peel was also aware of the firm hand. 'I always felt Michael Hurll was a bit of an authoritarian figure. The idea that he was the man who generated a party atmosphere – I don't remember him like that at all.'

'It got very serious,' says Richard Evans, who by this time was head of promotion at Epic Records. 'Very strict. There was none of this turning up late or drunk. You got there on time, and you did the show and you went. It became easier and harder in equal measure. But it worked. If the show hadn't got through that period of change, I don't think it would still be here today.'

'There was the party atmosphere on the show,' says presenter Mike Read, who was notorious for his bad time-keeping, 'but, on the other hand, I sometimes felt Michael Hurll was a bit of a taskmaster. I remember being about five minutes late one time. I said, "Mike, I'm really sorry I'm late," but he didn't book me for about three or four months after that.'

But, whatever his personal style, Hurll had a clear vision. 'The idea of putting a party atmosphere to the show,' he explains, 'was that the viewer felt they were part of the programme, that they were actually there enjoying it. Before, it had become very antiseptic and clinical.'

'When I took over *Top of the Pops*, I was going to make some changes,' says producer Michael Hurll ominously. 'We made it more like a party.' That simple word, 'party' set the tone for what *Top of the Pops* became.

First to go were the dancers. By the turn of the decade, Legs & Co were on their last legs. Flick Colby was the first to admit that the idea of an all-girl group had looked dated even before she reluctantly created them, but when Arlene Phillips came along on *The Kenny Everett Show* with the scandalous Hot Gossip, even those lecherous BBC bosses had to admit that wholesome girls-next-door Legs & Co were out of step. Flick was delighted when Hurll allowed her to bring in a more flexible and creative concept. 'They were called Zoo, and it was a group of about 20 different dancers, which would change every week depending on the record,' she explains. 'It meant you could do something which was actually relevant to the record.' Zoo – who debuted at the end of 1981 – included a whole range of dancers, some with street skills, some with classical training. One of them was a British disco dancing champion called Julie Brown, who earned a footnote in pop history when she went off to the States to become a huge celebrity as one of MTV's very first VJs.

But things didn't go smoothly for Zoo either. Flick Colby still directed the dance numbers from the gallery – the only part of *Top of the Pops* that Hurll didn't control – and she soon felt it had become a battle of wills. When Hurll arrived with a Page Three girl and insisted she should become a member of Zoo, Flick knew it was time to leave.

But the departure of Flick and her dancers – who one way or another had been integral to the show since 1968 – made little impact on Hurll's vision of *Top of the Pops*. His prime interest was in the audience. The set had been redesigned to place the crowd in the studio around and behind the bands, so they were in full view. The audience had always been part of the programme, but now they were right up there on screen nearly the whole time. They were given flags, hats, banners and balloons, and strict instructions to have a good time. 'It started to look like an American political convention,' says veteran Jimmy Savile, whose last days on the show were around this time. 'I didn't particularly agree with that. There were people saying, "Shout now" or "If you don't dance, you're out." They tried to treat the audience like they were professional dancers – "Do this" and "Do that" and "Don't stand there". The young people were getting regimented, to get them to do something that wasn't natural – and to me, it showed it wasn't natural. There were people diving in and out saying, "If you don't move more you won't get a ticket for next week." What was that all about?'

The fact that the show's original presenter found it unrecognizable is a measure of the

Top: As the decade went on, dancers were placed on podia and became known as 'cheerleaders'. Whoopee!

scale of Hurll's changes. But there was more to come. The money saved from Zoo was spent creating a new breed of TV stars, the 'cheerleaders'. Their job was to get the audience whooped up and responsive when the cameras were on them. The most enthusiastic were placed on podia. This really annoyed Jimmy Savile: 'For some inexplicable reason they had professional dancers in the audience, and they put the professional dancers on rostrums. It was obvious that they were professional dancers, they weren't the audience, they weren't being naturally exuberant. They were doing it because they were getting paid. That's not *Top of the Pops*, it's a presentation of manufactured glitz.'

Viewers from this era may recall seeing the same two blokes grinning at the camera week after week. Even the presenters were confused. 'At first, I used to think, how can these people be here every week?' says Janice Long. 'They're a bit sad. But then I realized they were the dancers. I think a lot of them were hoping it would be a route to fame and fortune.' For one of them, it was: Craig Fairbrass was a good-looking lad from Deptford when he joined as a cheerleader. Twenty years later he was back on primetime BBC1, playing *EastEnders* hard man Dan Sullivan.

'It was funny, really,' adds Janice. 'All those people going round trying to get everybody to dance. There were people with huge hairstyles and padded shoulders, all banging into each other. Lots of dancers who looked like they'd got wood-stain perma-tan on, doing this [strikes a pose]. It was funny standing there when it was going on, but it worked on the telly.'

There were important technical reasons for stage-managing the 'fun'. When *Top of the Pops* started going out live on a regular basis, the cheerleaders could guarantee an enthusiastic reaction. By this stage, the acts were all miming as well, so there was little or no interaction with the audience. 'We had to work really hard on the party atmosphere,' says Danny Steggall, who was working on the floor at this time. 'When you walk into an empty studio, it's such a sterile atmosphere. There was this big metal set with all the neon lights – it was very hit or miss as to whether it would come off. Then at the end when it was all over, there was this strange ritual where all the audience had to hand in their flags, balloons and deely-boppers to one of the staff.'

Eighties superstars

Of course, Hurll's era was also defined by the music. *Top of the Pops* played host to a colourful new breed of stars when the New Romantics emerged in 1981. Adam and the Ants, Wham! and Spandau Ballet all made their debut in that year, as did a bunch of Brummies called Duran Duran. Besides having an instant impact, their March 1981 debut with 'Planet Earth' was also a personal watershed for Simon Le Bon. 'It was a big breakthrough for me,' he says. 'Up until the time we did our first *Top of the Pops*, my dad had completely ceased any communication with me since he found

Below: Spandau Ballet were one of the first New Romantic bands on the show, with their November 1980 debut 'To Cut A Long Story Short'.

out I joined a band. And it was only when that first *Top of the Pops* was shown that my dad called up and I spoke to him for the first time since I joined Duran Duran. He said, "Well, I guess you're doing all right then Simon, aren't you?"'

Frilly shirts, sashes, big hair and make-up became the norm on *Top of the Pops* – and that was just the blokes. Then, in 1982, came the even more flamboyant Culture Club, who made their debut with 'Do You Really Want to Hurt Me?' on 28 October 1982. At rehearsals, Boy George looked a mess, totally hungover, with his long hair plaited and matted, so none of the crew was ready for the vision that stepped out of the dressing room for the recording – Boy George appeared in a flowing white nightdress, with bows in his hair and lavish make-up. 'We'd only found out the day before that we were on,' says George. 'When we got in the chart, we were told we weren't eligible for *Top of the Pops*. Then we got a call to say a slot had come up because Shakin' Stevens was ill. I roped in a couple of my mates, Jenny and Pat, to do backing vocals. They weren't singers, they just wanted to be on telly. It certainly made an impact. If I had £10 for every time a bloke's come up to me and said, "I thought you were a bird when I first saw you on *Top of the Pops*", I'd be a rich man now. I was really pleased it caused a bit of

controversy. After we did the show, our plugger got called in and was told, "We can't promote this record, what is it? Is it a bird, is it a plane, is it a drag queen? What is it?"' 'It' went on to front one of the biggest bands of the decade. 'Just think' says George, 'I probably owe my career to Shakin' Stevens.'

Possibly the most notorious clip ever of *Top of the Pops*, the one that is most quoted and chuckled about by pop fans, is from a September 1982 performance by Dexy's Midnight Runners. Kevin Rowland and his band of scruffs performed 'Jackie Wilson Said' in front of a giant blow-up photograph of the darts player Jocky Wilson. It's difficult to get to the bottom of this one, especially when it's passed into history as one of the favourite cock-ups of all time, but Hurll still insists it was deliberate, that it was meant to be a joke. 'I'll expose one *Top of the Pops* myth,' he says. 'Dexy's Midnight Runners were doing their song "Jackie Wilson Said", and when they came to do the show they said, "Would you put a slide up of Jocky Wilson for a bit of a laugh?" So we did. Afterwards people said we were idiots and we'd put the wrong picture up. But that's the story.' It may have been a deliberate error, but it's a measure of how humourless *Top of the Pops* appeared at the time that people are still willing to believe it was a cock-up, even to this day.

Above, left: Is it a bird…? Boy George causing gender confusion with his *Top of the Pops* debut in September 1982.
Above, right: Slide-show confusion – Dexy's Midnight Runners perform 'Jackie Wilson Said' in front of a blow-up of darts player Jocky Wilson.

▶▶ Suggs

Alias Graham McPherson, is the lead singer of Madness.

To be perfectly honest, I never thought I was going to be in a band, I wasn't one of those people who watched *Top of the Pops* and thought, 'God, wouldn't it be great to be up there.' I wasn't a great singer — and people today might tell you I'm still not — but I was very fortunate to bump into some people who did have those aspirations, i.e., Madness. So I never really dreamt of being on *Top of the Pops*. Although as a viewer, I found it really glamorous and used to watch it religiously, as we all did at that age. Roxy Music and David Bowie and Gary Glitter and Slade, and all those other glamorous people. I very specifically remember seeing Roxy Music — I think they were doing 'Virginia Plain' — I was very excited with all that glamour and men in make-up and stuff. I suppose the idea that was going around at the time was that these artists looked as though they were coming from outer space, that they had an 'other worldliness' to them. And Cockney Rebel I was very fond of as well, especially when Steve Harley was wearing a bowler hat, which was probably the reason why I started wearing one.

We made the record 'The Prince' on the Two Tone label and we were waiting in the Two Tone office in Camden to find out if we had got *Top of the Pops*, because the single had got to Number 16 in the charts, only to find out we hadn't, and that Secret Affair were being flown in specially by helicopter to take our place. But, fortunately, the following week we did get on the show, and it was with much excitement that we headed off to Wood Lane. I remember borrowing someone's shoes, because I didn't have any decent shoes, and buying a suit from Johnson's on the King's Road that I was very pleased about.

We got into trouble a lot after that first performance. Being the kind of extrovert people we were, we would sometimes get out of hand, and the fact that you were miming would often cause problems. I mean, Lee would be chewing chewing-gum when he was supposed to be doing the sax solo, and [the producer] Michel Hurll would come tearing down from the gallery to berate us with phrases like, 'You're an embarrassment to yourselves and the BBC.' And I almost expected him to say, 'And the Queen.' That was what it was like in those days — it was all very proper, and we had a constant running battle with Michael Hurll. In hindsight, obviously he was doing his job, and with seven of us tearing up and down the corridors, causing chaos, it was a very difficult job to do.

But it was a love-hate kind of thing, because Michael Hurll was always very generous to us as well. He would say for 'I Like Driving in My Car' — why not bring a car on to the set? Which was very unusual at that time. And then for 'Our House',

he built a very nice house for us! Which was lovely, and we lived in it for six years!

When we realized we could do whatever we liked — and because there were seven of us — there was a certain element of 'if I don't do something mad I probably won't get on the telly at all, it'll probably all just be Suggs'. So then Lee would suddenly turn up in a bumble bee outfit, and then Carl would be a sergeant major. The thing that we always prided ourselves on was being serious about being funny. If we were going to be policemen, we would really look like policemen. We would have a lot of fun in theatrical costumiers picking outfits.

I remember once we were doing 'Night Boat to Cairo' in our shorts and pith helmets and all that and on the next stage it was Morrissey doing 'Heaven Knows I'm Miserable Now'. And I suddenly thought, 'Oh my goodness, what am I doing here wearing a pair of shorts and a pith helmet?'

We'd often get five hours in between the rehearsal and the main performance, during which time anything and everything could happen. We'd be running around in these costumes up and down the corridors of the BBC. Then we discovered a bar upstairs. One side of the bar was open to the public, but on the other side was a better bar that was for BBC employees. There was an Irish guy on the door that used to let us in, and the beer was like 2p a gallon, and of course after three or four hours in there, we'd definitely be four sheets to the old whatnot.

There was often a great atmosphere when it was going out live, there would be the streamers and party hats and whooping and cheering. And you were on there with all the other bands who were your contemporaries, so The Specials would be there and perhaps Dexy's Midnight Runners. All throughout our career, all we were interested in was trying to make a dynamic performance and trying to have some fun, and *Top of the Pops* was what it was all about.

In the middle of 1983, there were great celebrations for the one thousandth edition – culminating in a huge party hosted by Richard Branson at his Kensington nightclub, the Roof Gardens. There was evidence, though, that pop's new royalty weren't exactly in the same groove as the old-school BBC. 'It was a bizarre experience,' says one invitee. 'Branson insisted on greeting everyone, and this long queue developed. You had old boys who'd been in the BBC for years, cameramen and sound men with beards and corduroys and sandals, all lining up next to The Thompson Twins and a load of cheerleaders, waiting to be greeted by Richard Branson. Very strange.'

By January 1984, British pop was a huge success story, with bands like Culture Club, Duran and Spandau selling bucketloads of records. A great chance, then, to celebrate another *Top of the Pops* anniversary – this time, the show's twentieth birthday. Yes, an opportunity for even bigger flags. The opening band on that anniversary show was a debut act, Frankie Goes to Hollywood, performing a song called 'Relax', and the grinning *Top of the Pops* was about to fall flat on its face once again.

It wasn't *Top of the Pops*, though, that banned Frankie's 'Relax'. It wasn't even DJ Mike Read, although he got the blame. Six days after Frankie's *Top of the Pops* appearance, Read announced on his breakfast show that he thought the lyrics were unsuitable. But by the time he took his moral stance, the decision had already been taken at the highest level that the record could not be played because of its references to oral sex and ejaculation. And *Top of the Pops*, which had shown it only a week before, had to toe the line and not play the tune, even when it reached Number One. As with the Sex Pistols in 1977, it was a moment when the show lost faith with the youngsters who bought the music. And this time, if anything, it seemed worse, as the ban appeared to be steeped in hypocrisy.

Of course, the Frankie ban was a passing blip. Through the rest of 1984, *Top of the Pops* was in full flow, riding high on the huge success of the New Romantics. That year's Christmas Show featured Duran Duran, Howard Jones, Nik Kershaw, Culture Club, The Thompson Twins, Wham!, Paul Young and the miraculously 'unbanned' Frankie Goes to Hollywood, with no less than three of their massive hits from that year, including the unexpurgated 'Relax'. But that programme also delivered one of the great events in *Top of the Pops* history, a shining, starry finale that, quaintly, just failed to pull off what it tried to do. 'The great moment of my life was Band Aid,' says Hurll. 'It was a Christmas show and we got together nearly everybody who had appeared in the original Band Aid record.' Note: *nearly* everybody.

There was a great mood that day. Bob

Above, left: Kim was the first Wilde to appear on *Top of the Pops* – her dad Marty's run of hits in the fifties and early sixties had ended by the time the show was born.
Above, right: Bananarama had hits throughout the eighties and appeared on the show 18 times during the decade.

►► Holly Johnson

Lead singer of Frankie Goes to Hollywood and solo artist.

I think the first time I saw *Top of the Pops* was in the sixties — I remember my sister screaming, 'Oh my god, they've got James Brown doing "Sex Machine".' I suppose I was hooked from then on. Seeing Marc Bolan singing 'Telegram Sam' with glitter under his eyes, and David Bowie singing 'Starman' a bit later on sort of lit my blue touch paper as a performer.

I had actually been in bands since I was about 16 and I'd seen all my friends go on *Top of the Pops* before me, like Echo and the Bunnymen and The Teardrop Explodes and other people from Liverpool. I kind of didn't believe it was going to happen to me, I was giving up music really. Then it was an appearance on The Tube that catapulted 'Relax' into the Top 40, which qualified us for a position on *Top of the Pops*. I remember being particularly worried that we might get recognized at the dole office, because we had no money. The record company were very stingy and we had to go to them and say, 'Look if we do *Top of the Pops*, we can't sign on any more, you have to put us on a wage.' So that was the most serious implication for me of being on *Top of the Pops*.

It was sort of exciting, although there's definitely two sides to the *Top of the Pops* experience. There's what you see on the screen, the glamour, the glitz, the fantastic pop stars, and then in the eighties there was the dreary canteen of BBC Television Centre and the extras from *Tenko*, that you had to share dressing-room spaces with. And the windowless dressing rooms that were really miserable and corporate, a bit like going back to school, somehow. It was all a bit officious, and very regimented, 'Oh no, you mustn't do this,' and 'You mustn't do that' and 'You must be here for a certain time'. But you could get your whole week's ironing done by the costume department. You just said, 'Oh, I don't know what to wear, could you iron all these things so I can decide?'

I remember the first *Top of the Pops* with 'Relax' vividly. I was introduced to Paul Gambaccini and he said, 'Gee, Holly, I'm amazed you've got away with this song.' He said, 'No one's got a direct reference to sex in a single since Lou Reed talks about giving head in "Walk on The Wild Side".' I didn't feel as though I was getting away with anything because the word 'cum' — although it's slang for ejaculation — it isn't actually a rude word in itself. It had already been played 90 times on Radio 1 before it was banned.

I thought there was really no good reason to ban it, especially after we'd performed it already on *Top of the Pops*. I thought it was hypocrisy. But who would I protest to? Mike Read? For me, the BBC was a completely faceless monolith. I think doubtless it contributed to the success of the record, not only in England but in other territories. We even started using it in the advertising — 'Frankie Goes to Hollywood: Big, banned and beautiful'. It gave the band a sort of cachet of rebelliousness.

Then, all of a sudden, because we'd had three Number Ones [during the rest of 1984] and we were the biggest band in the country at that particular time, they sort of sheepishly said, 'Oh well, we're going to let you do "Relax" on the Christmas *Top of the Pops*.' And we said, 'Oh really? Well, why couldn't we do it all year then?' It just seemed ridiculous to me. I think the producers thought they were being terribly outrageous in allowing us to do it, but I just thought it was foolishness.

With Frankie Goes To Hollywood, the visual aspect was always as important as the musical one. It was a theatrical event, and we wanted it to look special each time we were on television, to be different from the other groups. Frankie Goes To Hollywood didn't have dodgy haircuts, it just wasn't allowed. We left that up to Duran Duran and A Flock of Seagulls — they had really dodgy haircuts. Our performances aren't really that embarrassing when you watch them today. I felt Frankie came at the end of an era when you had quite visually aware groups like Duran Duran, Culture Club, Spandau Ballet, Wham!, and really we had to outdo them in a visual sense. We had to make them look safe and a soft option. Well, actually, that was easy, 'cos they were safe and a soft option. Especially Wham!

Geldof turned up with a pile of 'Feed the World' T-shirts over his arm, and insisted that everyone wear one, not just for 'Do They Know It's Christmas?', but also for their own tunes. He must have been so proud that Black Lace took him up on the offer for their performance of 'Agadoo'. When it came to the take – actually, it was two takes, as the programme was recorded on two consecutive nights – there were all the artists who'd appeared on the Christmas show, and more besides. Phil Collins, Jim Diamond, Status Quo, Bananarama, Slade, The Flying Pickets, Marilyn, Heaven 17, and the Frankie boys were all there to show their support in the chorus. But a couple of the lead vocalists – the ones who sing one line each of the verse – weren't present. Hurll insisted that Paul Weller step forward to mime to Bono's line. Despite Weller's protests, there was no question. 'There was a lot of argy-bargy,' says one witness, 'but in the end he was just told to do it.' Faced with the prospect of never doing the show again, Weller did his bit – or, rather, Bono's bit. Another slightly off-target *Top of the Pops* moment (but, hey, it was all for charity).

Madonna also made her debut in 1984 at a particularly memorable recording. She and Cyndi Lauper had flown over to the UK on the same plane, and they were both on *Top of the Pops*. Cyndi went mad for 'Girls Just Wanna Have Fun', running all over the set, up and down the stairs, even at one stage tapping out the instrumental break on the balcony railings with a pair of drumsticks. Madonna, in contrast, was coolness personified. Her act for 'Holiday' had been honed in the New York clubs, and suited the studio perfectly. Her routine included two dancers, her brother, Christopher, and her friend Erikah Belle. In December 1984, she appeared again for 'Like A Virgin', solo this time, but draped in a studded

leather jacket and eye-catching pink wig. 'I thought she was somebody totally different,' says Hurll. 'I actually ignored her and thought it was some mad woman coming round the studio.'

Top of the Pops around this time seemed to typify the mood of cheesy 'fun'. The Tony Blackburns and Noel Edmonds of the seventies had been replaced by the likes of Mike Read, Janice Long, Peter Powell and Gary Davies. But the tone remained the same, and the DJs put the same amount of enthusiasm into introducing each and every band.

'I suppose our heyday was ruled by the real Smasheys and Niceys,' says Suggs, lead singer of Madness. 'Your DLTs and Mike Reads, really funny blokes with terrible catchphrases. There was a real division between them and us – they were the real showbiz people and we were just the oiks who shouldn't really have been there as far as they were concerned. Most of them we got on with, but there was certainly that really old-fashioned idea of presenting.'

'It was cheesy wasn't it?' admits Janice Long, who says she was harangued into joining in the all-pervading 'fun'. 'I think I'm pretty hyper anyway, but they'd go, "Can you be livelier?" And then they'd go, "No, no, one more time ... livelier!"'

Generally, the Radio 1 jocks were happy to perform. For one thing, a slot on TV got them recognized, so they could earn more money for personal appearances. But, thankfully, there was at least one rebel in the ranks –

Top: Madonna performing 'Like A Virgin' on *Top of the Pops* in a bright pink wig. Above: Paul Weller and The Jam made history as the first act ever to have three singles enter the chart at Number One.

'It was good when John Peel presented, because you could tell he wasn't 100 per cent into some of the acts. He obviously couldn't say, "I personally think this group's rubbish," but he put so little enthusiasm into introducing some acts that you got the message.' JARVIS COCKER

the great John Peel. He'd been at Radio 1 for 14 years when he made his debut on *Top of the Pops* in 1982. His links, especially the ones when he was paired off with David 'Kid' Jensen, were some of the best TV moments of the eighties.

Peel appeal

'Basically, neither of us gave a toss about it,' says Peel. 'The others saw it as an important career move, somehow hoping to get their own chat show out of it. But I certainly didn't, so we rather took the mickey out of it.' Peel and Jensen used to order from the BBC's

Top: John Peel meets Kylie Minogue at *Top of the Pops* in 1988.
Below: A-Ha became Norway's most successful pop act ever.

costume department sombreros, seventeenth-century French courtiers' costumes, Blues Brothers outfits – basically, anything to look silly. They also came up with some great one-liners. Peel would earnestly announce a track that meant a lot to him after he'd played it on his evening show – cue Keith Harris and Orville; or, 'And now here's a band who put the Big in Big Country'; or, 'That record was the best thing since Napoleon's retreat from Moscow.'

The shows were often live, so producers had little control over what Peel said; for example, on 29 May 1986, he and Janice Long introduced Pete Wylie with 'Sinful'. 'If that doesn't make Number One,' Peel told viewers, 'I'm going to come round and break wind in your kitchen.' Looking back, Peel is amused by the reaction. 'It's not the kind of thing that gets into books of quotations,' he says. 'It's not even fantastically clever – but having said it on *Top of the Pops*, it attained this preposterous level of importance. Michael Hurll was in Australia, and apparently he was woken in the middle of the night, and alerted to the extra-ordinary danger to national security engendered by me making this remark about breaking wind in people's kitchens. I thought that this was hilariously funny – not the remark itself, but the consequences of it.' People complained, and *Top of the Pops* was told off by Anne Robinson on *Points of View*. 'Hurlly was great about it,' says Janice. 'He said, "Can you do anything else controversial? I love it when we get phone calls, 'cos it means people are watching!"'

John Peel brought more than a string of one-liners to *Top of the Pops*. He was clearly mocking the fake party atmosphere, but his presentation was a breath of fresh air and his efforts didn't go unnoticed by the fans, including the young Jarvis Cocker. 'It was good when John Peel presented,' says Jarvis, 'because you could tell he wasn't 100 per cent into some of the acts. He obviously couldn't say, "I personally think this group's rubbish," but he put so little enthusiasm into introducing some acts that you got the message. It was always a good laugh, being so deadpan in this supposedly party atmosphere.'

Sadly, Peel's contribution was short-lived. 'It was a funny sort of experience,' he says, 'because people would recognize you afterwards, but only for about two days, then you would slip back into oblivion again. I like oblivion – that's where I've spent most of my life. People would come up to me and say, "Are you the bloke off the telly?" And I thought, no I'm not really. The idea of being the bloke off the telly was most unattractive. So I just said I didn't want to do it any more.'

The Hit Factory

In July 1984 a song by Hazel Dean called 'Whatever I Do' slipped into *Top of the Pops* almost unnoticed. It was the first hit from three producers called Stock, Aitken and Waterman. The following February, another of their acts made a greater impact. No one could ignore Dead or Alive and their singer Pete Burns, an outrageous Scouser who made Boy George look like Marie Osmond. Pete was determined to enjoy his 15 minutes of fame.

'Pete turned up at *Top of the Pops* in a pair of golden shorts,' says his plugger, 'After dress rehearsal, I was summoned up to the gallery by Michael Hurll, who said, "You've got to do something about Pete Burns, because he's moving around too much in his shorts. Tape him down or something." So I took him down to the dear old BBC costume lady. She took one look and said she didn't want to go anywhere near him. So in the end we had to ask Pete to tape himself down with Sellotape.'

While Pete Burns was sorting out his trouser trouble, Stock, Aitken and Waterman were concentrating on the music, and proving they could make stars out of almost anyone. Next up was Page Three 'stunna' Sam Fox, who debuted on *Top of the Pops* in March 1986 with 'Touch Me (I Want Your Body)'. Later in the same year, Bananarama released their first PWL (Pete Waterman Limited) single, 'Venus'. The following year the Hitmakers made a record with their 'tea boy', Rick Astley, whose 'Never Gonna Give You Up' proved the

Above: The only way was up for Yazz after her *Top of the Pops* debut in July 1988. Four Top 20 hits followed.

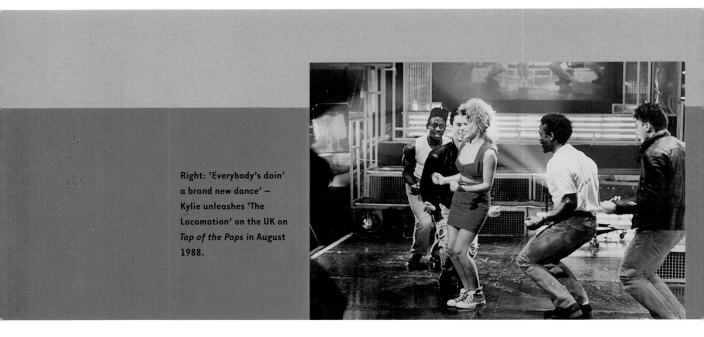

'When she walked on that *Top of the Pops* floor, the whole place lit up and she took over. If you look at her amazing, successful run, *Top of the Pops* leapt through the roof at that time because they loved each other. It was Kylie Pops.' PETE WATERMAN

producers' skills in marketing as well as production. First they released the record to radio and to the clubs and it became a huge hit. Pete Waterman waited until the record was at Number One before allowing him to do *Top of the Pops*. 'I knew that everyone thought that Rick Astley was black. When he walked in to *Top of the Pops*, and turned out to be a skinny little kid with red hair from the north of England, it blew people away. By the time he did *Top of the Pops*, he'd already done 240,000 singles. After he did *Top of the Pops* we suddenly did 95,000 in a day, because that was the power of that show.'

Stock, Aitken and Waterman soon found another star, the Australian actress Kylie Minogue, and discovered in her the perfect product. 'Kylie Minogue. Now you're talking about an artist who was so, so right for *Top of the Pops*,' says Waterman. 'It was the perfect combination.'

Kylie made her debut on the show in February 1988 in a specially shot promo for 'I Should Be So Lucky'. She couldn't make it to the studio because she was in Melbourne filming *Neighbours*, in which she was already a huge star. For the next release, 'Better the Devil You Know', she did turn up and it was a watershed. 'When she walked on that *Top of the Pops* floor, the whole place lit up and she took over,' says Waterman. 'If you look at her amazing, successful run, *Top of the Pops* leapt through the roof at that time because they loved each other. It was Kylie Pops.'

The product was bright and shiny, and the packaging was good. Part of that was the introduction of backing dancers. Madonna had done it before, but now they became a regular feature. 'We were the first to regularly put dancers on with pop stars,' says Waterman. 'The producers thought it was really novel that we turned up with four or five dancers. With that whole eighties thing, all the bands came in and performed and pretended it was real angst. So when we came on with five youngsters all dancing and smiling, it looked

fresh.' Kylie herself admits, 'I wasn't a very good live performer, so it was all about the routine. It was all about what it looked like.'

It was a winning formula, and the Hit Factory became a production line. Of course, there had been manufactured pop groups before, but Stock, Aitken and Waterman took the concept to new levels. In September 1988 Jason Donovan made his debut on the show, in July 1989 there was Sonia and, the following month, Big Fun. 'We never took *Top of the Pops* for granted,' says Waterman. 'We always knew you had three minutes to give it your greatest shot, and the whole combination of what we did was aimed at that three minutes on a Thursday night.'

The great moment of PWL's hit parade was, of course, 'Especially For You', Kylie and Jason's 1988 Christmas single. The making of the record had been a slapdash affair: Kylie and Jason had been reluctant to do it, keen to conceal the fact that they were lovers in real life. When he finally got the go-ahead, Waterman dashed to Australia to record the duet in between recordings of *Neighbours*. But there was no point releasing it unless the singers could come over and promote it on *Top of the Pops*. The two stars came more or less straight from the airport to perform that famous routine with hardly any rehearsal.

'The dance routine was left to the last minute,' recalls Waterman, 'and it didn't quite work. I remember going to *Top of the Pops* with it, and we hadn't got a clue what we were doing.' Nevertheless, with Kylie in her burgundy waistcoat and Jason in his leather jacket, it became a treasured *Top of the Pops* moment – and a Christmas Number One.

The machine that was Stock, Aitken and Waterman wasn't the only boost to *Top of the Pops* around this time. In 1987 the BBC struck a deal to show *Top of the Pops* in America. It only lasted for six months but during that time, a host of superstars started miraculously popping up on the show. Mick Jagger came on with a solo record 'Let's Work', for which he was allowed to run around all five stages in the studio. The Bee Gees did their comeback single, 'You Win Again', and Paul McCartney also sang the forgettable ditty 'Once Upon a Long Ago', twenty years after 'Paperback Writer' and 'Rain'. It was ironic to see all these

Above, left: Kylie and Jason, 'Especially For You' especially for *Top of the Pops* in December 1988. Above, right: Jason Donovan had the best-selling album of 1989, plus three Number One and two Number Two singles that year.

Above: Paul McCartney performing 'Once Upon A Long Ago' on *Top of the Pops* **in December 1987.**

started the trend in 1985 with '19'. By 1987 there was a Number One for M/A/R/R/S with 'Pump Up the Volume', and for S Express with 'Theme from S Express'. And for every Number One, there were dozens of smaller acts that made it to the lower end of the chart and had little to offer in the way of performance. 'People used to make the records in their front room or the garage,' says Michael Hurll, 'then they'd suddenly realize they were going to appear on *Top of the Pops*. I used to call them Job Centre bands because you felt that when they knew they were in the charts, they went down the Job Centre and said, "You first four go out there to *Top of the Pops* and do the so-and-so number."'

The new dance acts made the show look very strange and threw the spotlight on an age-old issue once more – miming. Under Thatcher, the grip the unions held on the BBC had, as elsewhere, eased. The MU rules about artists singing live had long gone. Now *Top of the Pops* had become a miming show again, only this time, it all seemed to be done very badly. 'Often, artists were so bad at miming that one had to do retake after retake till they could get themselves in sync,' says the show's director at the time, Brian Whitehouse. 'On a live show where there's no way you can do a retake, it makes the artist look a bit of a fool, and the public don't like it at all. Viewers felt they were being cheated, and they *were* being cheated.'

There was no worse example of such difficulties than Black Box's 1989 Number One, 'Ride On Time'. The record included an uncredited sample from soul singer Loleatta Holloway, and the story blew up while the record was Number One. The exotic Black Box frontwoman Katrin had to go on *Top of the Pops* and mime the vocal when everyone knew it wasn't her voice. *Top of the Pops* found it diffi-

acts finally returning to *Top of the Pops*. For so many years, they hadn't been available, and had only appeared on the show in their videos: even The Bee Gees had failed to mark their massive run of hits in the late seventies with a single *Top of the Pops* appearance. Now, they were suddenly queuing up to come on, all with a business eye to the American market.

Faceless dance

The PWL acts and the occasional superstars gave *Top of the Pops* a great boost at the end of the eighties. But then along came a new form of music that wasn't so TV-friendly. House music emerged from the clubs – for the kids, by the kids and, controversially, linked to drug culture. At its core were faceless, anonymous acts, but *Top of the Pops* could not ignore it because these records had a habit of flying to the top of the charts. Paul Hardcastle had

The faces, not the voices: Black Box (left) and Milli Vanilli (above). Neither act sang on their hit records.

cult to reflect the new, sampled world of house music, and incidents like this – plus the case of Milli Vanilli, who appeared on *Top of the Pops* in October 1988 miming to somebody else's voices – undermined the credibility of the programme as a whole. Dads everywhere were justified in shouting, 'Call that music? They can't even sing.' Miming on *Top of the Pops* had always been a subject of national debate in the UK, on a par with royalty and football, and now it provided old and young alike with the chance to slag off the show.

The issue came into sharp focus when the Great Miming Disaster of 1988 happened. It was a live programme featuring 'Martha's Harbour' by All About Eve. Someone, though, had tripped the power switch in the studio, and there was no sound coming out of the speakers that were supposed to cue the band. Singer Julianne Regan simply couldn't hear

the track, even though her song was being broadcast live to the nation. The cameras went through all their scripted moves while Julianne sat on her stool in a pool of dry ice, wondering what the hell was going on. 'She was inconsolable afterwards,' says her plugger, Martin Nelson. 'In floods and floods of tears. But they made it up to her, they invited her back the following week, and the record got to Number Three, which it probably wouldn't have done otherwise.' Great for All About Eve, but it made *Top of the Pops* look like a joke.

However, there was little alternative. In May 1988 New Order arrived to sing 'Blue Monday '88' and, as a credible band, they thought they'd make a point by playing live. *Top of the Pops* didn't do them any favours that day – the performance featured some of the worst live sound in history. 'Usually the sound department's biggest job was to hand out

wooden dummy microphones,' says one crew member, 'so to actually set up for a live band caused no end of problems. If you've seen the clip, you'll know it turned out as a complete disaster, and a memorial to how not to do live singing on TV.'

By the end of the eighties, producers were aware that *Top of the Pops* appeared out of touch with 'the kids'. Mirroring the situation 10 years earlier, when *Top of the Pops* didn't know how to deal with punk, the sudden change in the landscape left the show floundering somewhat. There wasn't very much that producers could do about the music, so they turned to the presenters. In 1988 the Radio 1 monopoly was broken, as names from the lower echelons of children's TV started appearing, in the hope that they'd be more in touch with teenage viewers. The likes of Andy Crane, Caron Keating, Susie Mathis and Anthea Turner started to front the show, even though they were relatively inexperienced and unfamiliar to many viewers. Not only faceless dance acts, but faceless presenters as well. What's more, they didn't necessarily do the job of bringing more credibility to the show. 'There was a band called KLF,' admits Anthea

Turner. 'I introduced them as KLM – which of course is a Dutch airline. But I wasn't allowed to go back and change it! Great advert though for the airline.'

One veteran presenter who was moved aside was Mike Read. 'I thought it was very strange when they started moving Radio 1 people off *Top of the Pops*,' he says, 'because we were familiar faces, familiar voices. But they started saying, "Hey, why don't we be a bit more street, a bit more cred and get some other people in?" It was like, "Oh well, anyone can present *Top of the Pops*."'

Competing for cool

It wasn't just changes in the music and presenters that caused people to think differently about *Top of the Pops* in the second half of the eighties: there was competition. Channel 4's *The Tube* ran between 1982 and 1987, as a kind of irreverent alternative to *Top of the Pops*. It attracted low audiences, but high awareness. In 1988, ITV put its big guns behind a direct competitor to the Pops, called *The Roxy* and presented by 'Kid', now 'David', Jensen. And if you'd forgotten *The Roxy*, you certainly won't remember *Switch*, *Network 7*, *Club X*, *Def II* or

Opposite and left: The Stone Roses and The Happy Mondays appeared on the same show on 23 November 1989. The Roses did 'Fools Gold' and Kirsty MacColl joined the Mondays for 'Hallelujah'.

the myriad of other shows that allowed Janet Street-Porter to claim she'd changed the face of youth TV. Many of these shows were short lived, none of them had mainstream impact (not at the time, anyway) or got anywhere near the ratings that *Top of the Pops* was still enjoying. Nevertheless, they clearly had an impact on perceptions, and forced the BBC constantly to re-examine *Top of the Pops*. But when the BBC tried to become cool like its rivals, they clearly got it wrong.

Head of Variety for the BBC by this the time was Jim Moir. 'Certainly we were conscious that other shows were being created which were making their mark on the public,' he says. 'It became fashionable to say, well it's "square", it's not "cool" to watch *Top of the Pops*.'

'The business was changing, the music was changing, television was changing,' says Anthea Turner. 'It was all part of a change for *Top of the Pops*.'

As the nineties dawned, the show was in a bad way. *Top of the Pops* had faced troubles before, but this time it was different. Now, threats like the new, 'cooler' youth shows and, indeed, music itself, were factors outside the control of the BBC. The viewers knew it,

the bosses at the BBC knew it – *Top of the Pops* seemed to be on its last legs. And, worst of all, no one seemed to have a clue what to do about it.

Left: Liza Minnelli's one and only appearance on *Top of the Pops* in August 1989, singing with the Pet Shop Boys. She refused to enter the studio unless she was allowed to smoke. Permission had to be sought from the highest authorities in TV Centre, and eventually she was allowed to light up – as long as there was a fire officer following her round with a bucket of sand.

SPANDAU BALLET were one of the first New Romantic bands on *Top of the Pops*. Between 1980 and 1986 they had 15 Top 20 hits.

FRANKIE GOES TO HOLLYWOOD performed 'Relax' on the 20th anniversary show, but were banned a week later when the BBC realized what the song was about.

ELVIS COSTELLO photographed at *Top of the Pops* in 1981 performing 'A Good Year for the Roses'. He had been a regular on the show since the days of punk, and was one of the few acts to survive the era.

GRACE JONES performing 'Private Life' on the show in August 1980. Other hits on the show that week were David Bowie's 'Ashes to Ashes' and ABBA's 'Winner Takes It All'.

MADONNA backstage at *Top of the Pops* in January 1984, the month she first stepped on to the world stage with 'Holiday'. She is seen here with her regular dancers, Erikah Belle and her brother, Christopher Ciccone.

LISA STANSFIELD making her debut on *Top of the Pops* in February 1989 with 'People Hold On'. Like Yazz, her first hit was as vocalist for Coldcut, but she went on to have huge solo success around the world.

SIOUXSIE SIOUX in full flight with the Banshees on *Top of the Pops*. She made her debut on the show in 1979 with 'Playground Twist' and went on to make nine appearances during the eighties.

THE EURYTHMICS had twelve Top 20 hits between 1983 and 1988. Despite favouring videos to promote their songs, they still made six appearances in the *Top of the Pops* studio.

KYLIE MINOGUE in rehearsals on 31 October 1989, ready to perform 'Never Too Late'. She was one of the first acts to have dancers on stage with her.

IAN BROWN performs with The Stone Roses on 21 November 1989. It was a memorable day for fans of Madchester, as The Happy Mondays were also on the show.

1990s

Many of the things that define the nineties are clearly visible on *Top of the Pops*. Think of Take That and, besides the songs of course, you think of the finely honed and ruthlessly efficient marketing package that couldn't have existed in previous decades. Then there was Britpop and its attendant lad culture. For the girls there was Girl Power and the Spice Girls' message of sexy self-assertion. *Top of the Pops* may have been in a bad way at the start of the nineties, but as we shall see, it bounced back, and once again rode on the waves of social change. What's more, *Top of the Pops* in the nineties set its sights on broader horizons. The show became a brand — and set out to conquer the world. Nowadays, New York taxi drivers, teenagers in Naples, Australian bushmen and waitresses in Singapore all know *Top of the Pops*. For a show that was nearly taken off the air at the beginning of the decade, *Top of the Pops* didn't do too badly in the nineties.

Above: Robbie Williams guest-presenting in September 1995. Opposite, top: Blur. Opposite, bottom: The Spice Girls.

Acts must sing live

At the start of the nineties, *Top of the Pops* was unable to challenge the 'cool' of other youth shows and was stuck in a quagmire of faceless dance acts. 'During the early nineties, the record industry was getting very worried and concerned about *Top of the Pops*,' says Martin Nelson, one of the most senior promoters in the business. 'The audience was dropping, it was being booked almost by rote, regardless of whether the act had any ability to perform. The audience were voting with their hands and switching over.'

Head of BBC Variety, Jim Moir, echoes these thoughts: 'There was definitely concern within the BBC that its ratings dominance was beginning to ebb, and it was very difficult to understand what precisely to do about it.'

Week to week, the producers were floundering. 'Television was advancing rapidly,' says Stan Appel, who'd started on the show as a cameraman in 1966, and who'd finally worked his way up to the job of producer. 'But our programme was done very quickly, and we didn't have vast budgets. The show wasn't advancing, it wasn't ahead of its time. You were just very keen on keeping the programme going just as it was. It stood still, perhaps.' But, in October 1991, there was change, and something the viewers couldn't fail to notice. In a brave attempt to restore some kind of credibility to the show, a new rule was introduced that all the acts had to sing live. It was a seismic shift in the programme's approach, and had devastating effects.

The new rule was made possible when *Top of the Pops* moved out of Television Centre, its home for 25 years, to the BBC's Elstree studios, 30 miles outside London. BBC Elstree is a sprawling campus that, since 1985, had been home to *EastEnders*. The new *Top of the Pops* studio could house a permanent set – unlike TV Centre, where it had to be dismantled and built afresh every week – but, most importantly, they built a proper sound system at Elstree. At last, *Top of the Pops* could have the feel of a live gig and no one would be allowed to mime.

'I got fed up with everybody miming,', says Appel, who introduced the rule. 'I got feedback that the public didn't like to be conned.' But his new rule came at exactly the wrong time for many performers. Many of the polished pop acts of the era fell flat on their faces as they attempted live vocals. Particular stinkers were performed by Bananarama and Dannii Minogue. When Duran Duran staged a mini-comeback with 'Ordinary World', they were highly entertained by how different it was from their heyday. 'You'd get people who could sing, but you'd also get people who really couldn't sing,' says Simon Le Bon. 'It was quite horrific listening to it back. These people were trying desperately to sing in tune, and it's like, "Ooh, go back to miming, darling."'

'Everyone was forced to sing live if they wanted to appear on the programme,' says Martin Nelson, 'and obviously not everybody is capable of producing a perfect live performance in the environment of the *Top of the Pops* studio. So some performances were better than others – and some were just awful. It wasn't very fair on the artists at all, especially if they were a studio act with no experience of

'There was definitely concern within the BBC that its ratings dominance was beginning to ebb, and it was very difficult to understand what precisely to do about it.' JIM MOIR

Left: In November 1991, a sore throat forced Kurt Cobain of Nirvana to sing 'Smells Like Teen Spirit' an octave lower than usual in their live *Top of the Pops* performance.

singing live in front of an audience. But they were expected to do it.'

The immediate effects on the programme were not entirely positive. Many fans didn't want to see their cheery little pop favourites being made fools of, and the record industry didn't appreciate the extra effort involved in turning pop stars into proper live acts. Many acts simply refused to turn up, so *Top of the Pops* was forced to show more and more videos, resulting in the exact opposite to the 'live event' feel the programme was trying to create.

One of the first bands to come up against the new rules was a debut group from Seattle called Nirvana. They'd played an amazing live performance of 'Smells Like Teen Spirit' on *The Word* the previous week and they were expected to do the same on *Top of the Pops*. Unfortunately, Kurt Cobain was already well into the rock 'n' roll lifestyle – he'd been out on the town and his voice was completely shredded. So he asked to mime. 'Not on this show,' came the answer. He was told if he couldn't sing live, he couldn't do the show. So, reluctantly, he went on and sang his song an octave lower than the recorded version, and without the famous screams in the chorus. Inadvertently, it became another famous *Top of the Pops* moment when the song ended with what was officially the first spontaneous stage invasion in the *Top of the Pops* studio.

The presence of Nirvana, the wildness of a stage invasion: in some ways, *Top of the Pops* was trying to emulate the excitement that its rivals like *The Word* created. But it never really achieved it. After all, there was a huge difference between a late-night Channel 4 programme and a primetime BBC1 family show. The Red Hot Chili Peppers were left in no doubt about this when they showed up to perform their Top 10 hit 'Give It Away'. The band was famous at the time for appearing nude in photo shoots, with only a sock over their genitals. Their outfits for *Top of the Pops*,

Above: Take That helped to revive the fortunes of *Top of the Pops* in the early nineties, as the charts moved away from grunge and faceless dance acts.

completely see-through white dresses that left nothing to the imagination, were hardly less modest. 'During rehearsals, it was obvious they were taking the piss,' says one member of the crew who worked on both *The Word* and *Top of the Pops*. 'It would have been great on *The Word*, but not on *Top of the Pops*. They were grabbing their privates at the camera. It was obvious we just couldn't show it.' They refused to tone it down, and so were thrown off the programme. 'It was my worst experience with a group on *Top of the Pops*,' says Appel. 'They didn't want to alter anything, so I said, either they alter it or they go home now – and they went home.' It was clearly impossible for *Top of the Pops* to achieve anything like the cool of its rivals.

Fresh faces

Thankfully, as the nineties rolled on, the music did start to revive. 'Back when we started, there were loads and loads of faceless dance acts,' says Robbie Williams. 'It was all grunge and dance music. When we came along, music went from being dull to being dumb.' Dumb maybe, but the five pretty boys from Manchester known as Take That were a godsend for *Top of the Pops*. At last, there was a buzz about music again. Take That made their debut on the show – singing live – in June 1992, and regularly delivered what the show desperately needed. Excitement.

But even the young, fresh-faced Robbie noticed that there was a distinct lack of excitement at the BBC. 'Everybody that worked behind the cameras looked so bored,' he says. 'And I couldn't figure it out why they weren't excited to be working at *Top of the Pops* – 'cos I was. Doing your song was like waiting to go in and have your teeth removed.'

Sadly, Take That could not single-handedly revive the fortunes of *Top of the Pops*. If anything, the appeal of Take That took the show's average age down to early teens. Week to week, it was still bland and unfocused, and the presenters had gone from bad to worse. By now, the show had been colonized by a series of largely unknown children's TV presenters such as Toby Anstis, Mark Franklyn, Adrian Rose and Claudia Simon. Senior figures at the BBC admit that by 1993 they were ready to put *Top of the Pops* out of its misery. But there was another option, and they had nothing to lose by trying something completely different. 'I realized that we needed to bring a fresh attitude to the production of the show,' says Jim Moir. On a tip-off from concerned insiders from the record industry, he found the man he was looking for. 'I approached a Radio 1 producer, Ric Blaxill, who had innovative ideas, and he eventually agreed to move from Radio 1 to *Top of the Pops*.'

Younger blood

Ric joined *Top of the Pops* in February 1994. He was in his mid-twenties and taking over from a man who'd been working on the programme since before he was born. A passionate music enthusiast, Ric had already had great success as producer of Simon Mayo's Radio 1 breakfast show, making it sharp, lively and compulsive listening. He was charged with bringing the same qualities to the ailing *Top of the Pops*. 'As a music fan I would always watch the programme,' says Blaxill. 'But I thought there wasn't enough variety in the show, and the presentation was a little flat considering it was supposed to be an event. Obviously, there was concern from the record industry that this great show which could get their acts seen on TV was under some kind of threat. I was told that it might possibly be moved to BBC2 or even removed from the schedules.'

'We needed an attitude, which Ric could bring,' says Moir. 'The audience needed to see that there was something different happening on *Top of the Pops*.'

The week before he officially joined, Ric attended Stan Appel's last show. He says the Number One that week summed up his impression of *Top of the Pops*: it was D:Ream's 'Things Can Only Get Better'. 'We knew he was going to give the show a good kicking,' says warm-up man Danny Steggall. 'For the music fans in the crew, this was great, because we knew that was what it needed. But there were still a lot of BBC time-servers around who were just looking for an easy life. When this guy came along who'd never made a TV show before, they weren't too impressed.

He really had to assert himself, and he certainly took control. But he had a job to do. He'd been brought in to save it.'

In the couple of years prior to Ric's arrival, *Top of the Pops* had found a new way of dealing with the age-old problem of bands being unavailable because of tour commitments. They'd film a live performance, usually at record-company expense, on location at one of the gigs. Ric took the idea and turned it into a regular feature, known as 'the satellites'. He wanted them to become a talking point, and encouraged record companies to put their acts in more and more striking locations. These performances – Diana Ross at the Motown Museum in Detroit, Etta James on a boardwalk in Florida, Richard Marx from the Capitol Building in Washington – were flagged up as 'live via satellite' and, extraordinarily, they usually were. Even though *Top of the Pops* was pre-recorded, Ric wanted to add to the sense of occasion by going over live during the recording to wherever the location was.

'The easy option would have been to show the video,' says Blaxill, 'but the whole point of creating this sense of event around *Top of the Pops* was to say look, bands think this programme is so important to them that they actually want to create a special performance just for you, the *Top of the Pops* audience.'

One band who really took to the idea of satellites was Bon Jovi, creating a sense of occasion and drama whenever they did one. For 'Something for the Pain', they showed off the ultimate rock 'n' roll accessory, by performing on the tarmac in front of the Bon Jovi jet, which rolled up at the start of the song. No expense was spared. Another release coincided with the birth of Jon Bon Jovi's baby, Jesse James, so he didn't want to leave his home in New Jersey. Instead, the record company hired the local Giants football

Below: Bon Jovi perform live via satellite from Niagara Falls.

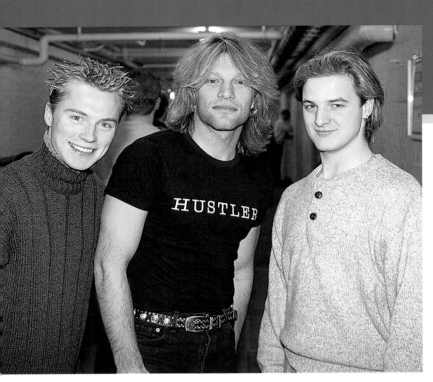

stadium, placed the band on the touchline, and shot the whole performance from helicopters flying overhead.

But the most spectacular was for 'Always'. Again, Jon wasn't available for the studio because he was filming in Canada with Whoopi Goldberg and the nearest US location happened to be on the border at Niagara Falls. 'We got the band's lighting engineers to light the whole Falls,' says promotions man, Martin Nelson. 'Jon was only with us for 15 minutes, then straight back to continue filming up in Toronto. It was a sensational piece of television.'

'The Niagara Falls one should have won an Oscar,' agrees Blaxill.

Guest presenters

Stunts like this were pure rock 'n' roll, and helped give the impression that things were happening at *Top of the Pops* again. But the presentation also needed a new look – and Blaxill took a radical approach. He got rid of the TV apprentices who had failed to set the show alight, and went straight to the other end of the scale. He threw the show open to big-name celebrity guest presenters.

'I wanted to create a sense of event around the presentation,' he explains, 'I used a variety of celebs from pop stars to sports stars to actors to comedians, so that in the 10-second link between every song, that was almost as unpredictable as what could happen on the stage with the bands.'

He knew the stars he booked would get people talking: Jarvis Cocker, Ant & Dec, Dale Winton, Frankie Dettori, Kylie Minogue, Damon Albarn, Meatloaf and Phill Jupitus were among many who held the golden microphone. One of Ric's idols, footballer Ian Wright, also did it, and had his hair dyed blond specially for the occasion. 'They could say what they liked,' says Blaxill, 'as long as they mentioned the band's name at the end of the sentence.'

The result was entertaining, but often unpredictable. The first time Jarvis Cocker took on presenter duties, he annoyed Michael Hutchence by calling his band 'Inks', saying it was 'a stupid name for a group'. 'Then there was that band called Let Loose on,' recalls Jarvis, 'and I tried to make some vague reference to farting, by saying, "I think somebody's Let Loose in here." I enjoyed it, it was my small contribution to modern culture.'

Even with links written by Ric Blaxill, Ant & Dec managed to upset the formidable Courtney Love and her band Hole. Courtney was already slightly 'on edge' that day – she'd brought her own doctor with her, and she had to be carried from the dressing room to the stage. When Ant & Dec introduced her as 'Kurt Cobain's widow', she stopped her performance and started regaling the bemused presenters, threatening to walk off the show if they said it again.

Ric's attempts to be risqué sometimes backfired. Comedian Paul Kaye, alias Dennis Pennis, was allowed to write his own links, which were in keeping with Pennis's 'insult-a-celeb' style. Fans of Skunk Anansie were not amused when they heard their favourite band introduced with the words, 'These guys are

called Skunk because they're black and white and they stink!' Pennis introduced Roxette by saying, 'They're from Sweden, where the men all have beards, and the women are clean shaven.' And when he said in the link that Chris De Burgh looked like a mole, the monitors in the studio had to be turned down so the 'Lady in Red' legend couldn't hear the comment as he began singing his brand-new hit.

But the guest presenter who's best remembered is undoubtedly boxer Chris Eubank.

'At the time there was a lot of friction with me and the public,' says Eubank. 'I used to enthral and infuriate at the same time. Also, everyone was playing on my lisp at the time, and I was always trying to prove that I don't have a lisp.'

For some reason, the script that day included numerous words beginning with the letter S. Sleeper, for example, with 'Sale of the Century' – an exclusive. 'In rehearsal, Chris actually asked me, "Are you trying to wind me up?", remembers Blaxill. 'I said, "No, of course not."' Another act was Suggs ... with 'Cecilia' ... at Number Six. Eubank decided to go for it. 'Here's a special song, by a special performer,' he announced. 'It's Suggs singing "Cecilia".' 'It was very difficult to sing the song with a straight face,' recalls Suggs.

The guest presenters were a novelty on *Top of the Pops*, and the novelty soon wore off. But on the whole, the guest presenters succeeded in drawing attention to the show and changing perceptions, and they provided some memorable moments, both good and bad.

Britpop

As ever, though, the main interest in *Top of the Pops* lay in the music, and Ric was fortunate that his arrival on the show coincided with the great revival in British music that became known as Britpop. 'It was an exciting time,' says

Jarvis Cocker of Pulp. 'Suddenly, the indie charts became the real charts, and there was a sense of excitement that this stuff has gone into the mainstream, and it was going to make a difference.'

The Britpop boom provided some classic moments; for example, when Damon Albarn was guest-presenting, and found himself introducing Oasis's 'Whatever'. 'We positioned him right in front of the stage,' says Blaxill, 'and the Gallaghers are there and Damon's doing his best to introduce them. But there were quite a few hand signals going up from the Gallaghers behind Damon's head. I think we had to go back and do that about five or six times.'

'I lived in a perpetually ironic state at the time,' recalls Damon Albarn. 'You go through a period when you're so hungry just to try anything. I would never do it again, not in a million years would I want to present *Top of the Pops*. But I did it then. I didn't do it very well. I don't regret it, but I'm not in any way proud of it.' But the Blur frontman still feels that *Top of the Pops* is an important show for his band. 'That's why we've always done *Top of the Pops*, because hopefully when we're doing something interesting, it gets us out to an audience which would never hear what we're doing unless we did that kind of show. I've always felt quite passionate about doing those mainstream things, even though most of the time, I loathe 90 per cent of the music on there.'

In August 1995 Britpop excitement came to a head as both Blur and Oasis released singles on the same day. Blur's 'Country House' won out, and their appearance in the Number One

Top: Ant and Dec present the show despite a run-in with Courtney Love. Below: Boxer Chris Eubank drew much comment when he took up the golden microphone.

Above: Damon Albarn's efforts as guest presenter were hampered by the bad behaviour of Oasis.
Right: Red leather day – Scary Spice Melanie B tries a new look for her 1998 debut solo single, 'I Want You Back'.

slot at the end of *Top of the Pops* was like watching the medal ceremony at the end of the Olympic 100-metres final. 'That whole period really wasn't very pleasant,' says Damon. 'It became something totally out of our hands, very odd indeed.' He might have found it odd, but for *Top of the Pops* it was bread and butter.

Girl power

As if Britpop wasn't enough, the following year saw a new phenomenon that was like manna from heaven for the show: a band that could have been custom-made for *Top of the Pops*, with looks, attitude, personality and great tunes – running on high-octane Girl Power. The Spice Girls' first appearance with 'Wannabe' was via satellite from Japan in July 1996. The following week it was Number One, and the girls were in the studio to celebrate. It remained at the top for a further six weeks, and they came back no less than three times. 'They always made themselves available,' says Blaxill, 'and always made their mark.' They were quick to cast the Spice spell over everyone they met. 'They all used to flirt with the crew and remember our names,' says one of the team who worked on the floor. 'All the guys definitely thought they were up for a shag with one of the Spice Girls.'

Ric used the new buzz around *Top of the Pops* to draw in some old favourites who hadn't been on for a while. 'Suddenly you had people like Stevie Wonder and Diana Ross coming back on the show. And out of nowhere we got Kate Bush and Morrissey and Elvis

Costello – all people that had said they'd never do it again. Mariah Carey was always available to come over and Bryan Adams was suddenly back on the show. And you're thinking, this show is achieving something. It became the must-see event of the week.' Ric mentioned in an interview in *Q* magazine that his biggest ambition was to get Paul Weller back on *Top of the Pops*. Paul read it and rang up to say he'd do it. Ric let him do two numbers, 'The Changingman' and 'Peacock Suit', back to back in June 1996. The Sex Pistols, who'd never appeared during their heyday, were also given the honour of doing two tunes later the same month, making their debut as they prepared for their 'Filthy Lucre' reunion tour. Again, it was a huge statement to have Johnny Rotten singing 'Pretty Vacant' live on *Top of the Pops*.

Blaxill and *Top of the Pops* were on a roll. 'You'd get shows some weeks when you'd have the Spice Girls on and Oasis on and Prince on, and in one instance, Madonna on, and you're

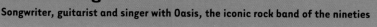
When I was young, I never got to go to gigs or anything like that. So *Top of the Pops* was where it all started for me.

My mam was into Pan's People and Legs & Co and all that stuff. It was a family thing. I remember saying to my mam about The Smiths, because The Smiths never used to put their pictures on the cover of the records. So when The Smiths came on *Top of the Pops*, I said, 'This is the guy I was telling you about.' And my mam said, 'What's wrong with him? Waving his flowers about'. And I said, 'That's his thing, that's what he does.'

I came to *Top of the Pops* once when the Inspiral Carpets were on. It was at Television Centre, and my job was just to get the amps plugged in, check the red light went on, then go off and get drunk. It was the best job in the world. But I used to stand somewhere off camera, then go home and watch it, and go, 'There's me.' And I'd pause the video and say, 'you can't actually see me, but you see that shadow – that's me!'

The first ambition of Oasis was to get a record deal, the second was to make a record, and the third was to be on *Top of the Pops*. Then with 'Shakermaker' [Oasis's first appearance in June 1994], it was incredible to have a Radio 1 DJ say, 'They're brothers and they're from Manchester,' and to mention your band's name. Bruno Brookes introduced us, and Liam said something to him, because during rehearsals he was saying something about a 'top indie band'. And Liam went over and said, 'We're not a f**king indie band, we're a rock 'n' roll band.' So when Bruno Brookes went on, he said something to the effect of, 'They're Oasis, and they're not an indie band, they're a rock 'n' roll band.'

It was our own idea to have Liam stand at the back for the performance of 'Shakermaker'. When you see The Sweet on *Top of the Pops*, or The Glitter Band or The Faces, the drummer is always down at the front. They had us on a stage that stepped up, so we stuck Liam at the back. It was a throwback to the seventies thing with Slade and T. Rex and all that stuff.

For 'Rock 'n' Roll Star', we got a call saying, you're doing *Top of the Pops*. And we said, 'We haven't got a single out, what song are we doing? "Rock 'n' Roll Star".' Me being a pop historian, I was like, 'But it's not a single.' I think we were the first band to do that with an album track. I remember buying a brand-new guitar for the occasion, as well. I don't know if anyone's ever noticed, but every time I was on *Top of the Pops*, I'd use a completely different guitar for the simple reason I figured that if I used them on television, especially on *Top of the Pops*, they'd then become infamous and they'd be worth more money. There's another one I used for 'D'You Know What I Mean?'. It was the white Rickenbacker that Paul [Weller] had

given me for my thirtieth birthday, the one he used in the video for 'Town Called Malice'. He literally used it, then put it in the case and never touched it for years, then gave it to me for my birthday. So I used it for 'D'You Know What I Mean?' That's a serious piece of memorabilia.

They always say, 'Do you want to sing live on *Top of the Pops*?" And we always say, f**k that. We're like, 'If you want us to sing, we want paying.' We've never played live on *Top of the Pops*, for the simple reason that we always treat it as a day out, and fun. We never really wanted to go there and be bothered about what it sounded like, or whether we'd played it wrong. Liam's miming is fantastic. The miming on 'Cum On Feel the Noize' is something we have a laugh about every time we see it. But we've been critically acclaimed as the best live band in the world twice, so we've got nothing to prove in the live stakes. At the point where we were the biggest group in the world, we treated *Top of the Pops* as a day off. We used to long for the days when you could go through those gates at Elstree, turn off all the communication systems, and just go and get pissed in the bar, knowing you were just going to have to go on and mime on the programme. And *Top of the Pops* to me was always fun. It's not meant to be work.

We were on it with Blur a couple of times. One time, we were walking past the make-up room – and we never wear make-up on the telly. We're like, tell it like it is, if you've got a spot on your forehead, then there you go. And we walked past the make-up room, and there were Blur, all in a line, getting their make-up done. So Liam – diplomat that he is – stuck his head round the door, and went, 'You look f**king gorgeous.' And I think that's where it all started. 'Cos we relentlessly bated them all day. 'Oh, your make-up's running, luv.' 'I think your mascara's running there, Damon.'

There was the time that I mimed Liam's part on 'Roll With It', and he mimed playing the guitar. It was the day we'd found out that some of the barcodes on the single were wrong, and they weren't going to register for the chart. We were all pretty drunk and we were all knackered, and all the thing with Blur had got completely out of hand. We felt that Creation had let us down a bit. I don't know why me and Liam swapped instruments, but if I'd known he'd mime guitar so badly, I wouldn't have bothered.

It's *Top of the Pops* – it's that brand name, it's that logo. It's where I learned to play music. It's where I got the ideas for how bands should be. That was where we copied it all from. It's part of your growing up, like riding a bike or playing football. You'll always have a soft spot for *Top of the Pops*. We still say, 'How are you feeling? I'm *Top of the Pops*, man!' We still say it to this day.

Right: Madonna chose a Morticia Addams look for her November 1998 performance of 'Power of Goodbye'.
Opposite page: The first edition of the *Top of the Pops* magazine tried to cover pop and indie, and brought Tony Mortimer of East 17 together with Brett Anderson of Suede.

sitting there in the gallery and you can't even believe it yourself that all these artists are gathered in the studio for *Top of the Pops*.'

A new night

Just as things were going so well the BBC intervened and pulled the rug from under the show just as it was back on form. In September 1996 *Top of the Pops* was moved from Thursday nights to Friday nights. It seemed like an arbitrary decision – apparently, the show wasn't 'performing' well against *Emmerdale*, so they decided they might as well stick it up against *Coronation Street*. For millions of viewers, it was ingrained in the consciousness that *Top of the Pops* was on a Thursday. Many of the younger ones

spent Friday nights getting ready to go out. The record industry, too, was horrified as the plug on Thursdays meant people would go out on Fridays to buy the records. With the Friday show, they only had Saturday to qualify for that week's Top 40. 'Moving *Top of the Pops* from a Thursday to a Friday night has changed the whole way British music is sold,' says Pete Waterman. 'No matter what the BBC thinks, it ain't the same.' The BBC, of course, would say *Top of the Pops* doesn't exist to promote the record industry, but the show had always relied on the industry's support, and the move came as a blow. 'You found that record companies were not investing quite so much money in the programme by that point,' says one senior plugger.

Becoming a brand

Nevertheless, Ric and the BBC had one or two more tricks up their sleeves. The corporation's commercial arm suddenly became interested in the UK pop revival, and launched *Top of the Pops* magazine, which soon made its mark. It was editor Peter Lorraine, not some anonymous marketing man, who first christened the Spice Girls Posh, Sporty, Ginger, Scary and Baby. The names first appeared in *Top of the Pops* magazine, and quickly became a key part of the Spices' marketing operation. The magazine started by trying to cover the whole range of music from the show, from guitar bands to rock to pop, but it soon became clear that the best strategy was to go for the *Smash Hits* teen market head on. By the end of the decade, it had overtaken its rival to become the biggest music title in the UK.

In 1994, *Top of the Pops 2* first appeared on BBC2. It began as a kind of overflow for the main show, playing a mix of new and established bands, padded out with archive, and presented by veteran DJ and muso, Johnnie Walker. It soon became apparent, though, that the archive was the most popular feature, and

when it became a back-to-back oldies format, with a mockingly affectionate commentary from Steve Wright, another hit show was born.

Flushed with his success, Blaxill had begun expanding *Top of the Pops* into new areas. In BBC terms, it was now a 'brand', a marketable commodity. There were to be further huge strides in this area in the coming years, but not under Blaxill. The pop explosion that had contributed so much to the success of the show prompted ITV to create its own version for Saturday mornings. It was Blaxill who launched *CD:UK* as the main rival to *Top of the Pops*. But he left the BBC show in immeasurably better shape than he found it.

'When Madonna turned up, she hadn't done the show for ages. She turned up with just a manager and a security guy. We were just about to shoot the show and he walked into the studio, put his arm around someone in the audience and just kind of guided them away. And you're thinking, what's going on there? So I asked him and he said, "That guy. If Madonna sees that guy, she'll freak, he follows her everywhere." He'd paid £100 outside to some school kid. But the security guy saw him instantly and kind of whisked him away.' RIC BLAXILL

Above: Boyzone were part of the pop explosion of the mid-nineties, helping the fortunes of both the show and the *Top of the Pops* magazine.

The Cowey era

His replacement also had a rock 'n' roll sensibility, and wasn't afraid to cause a stir. Chris Cowey brought his own unorthodox style to the show. He had cut his teeth as a researcher on *The Tube* in the mid-eighties, produced a live music show for Channel 4 called *The White Room*, and had overseen a number of Brit Award ceremonies. Unlike Blaxill, he was also a director.

Blaxill had cleared his desk immediately after resigning, so when Cowey first walked into the *Top of the Pops* studios at Elstree in mid-1997 there had been an interregnum of some weeks. The caretaker team were following the BBC tradition of camera scripting, where the song is broken down line by line, and each shot is pre-planned. It's a laborious but 'safe' process. One of the acts that week was Rosie Gaines, a big soul mama with a big

soul voice, who relished the chance of doing a live version of her hit 'Closer Than Close'. But in rehearsals she gave a little too much – her improvisations meant that the crew lost their places in the script. The director came down and told her she'd have to mime to the song so they could shoot it correctly, and the artist went back to her dressing room in tears.

The following week, Chris officially took the reins – and his first booking was Rosie Gaines. He defied convention by asking her to come and sing live the next week, exactly as he'd seen her in the previous week's rehearsals; he then tore up the camera scripts and told the cameramen to get in there and search out the best shots – much to their delight. 'We knew immediately it was going to be different,' says one of the crew. 'Because Chris is a director as well, he has the confidence to sit there and wing it. The whole thing becomes more relaxed and more spontaneous. Chris looks more like a roadie than a producer. He's the kind of guy you know will hate BBC politics, but he'll love his crew.'

Cowey decided to sweep away many of the Blaxill trademarks he saw as gimmicks. 'It was a kind of back-to-basics approach,' he says. 'I stripped away things like having guest presenters every week, who were really just trying to promote themselves. I wanted the music to speak for itself and cram as many bands as possible into the half hour. We really tried to keep it very simple and very basic.' Cowey's affection for what many see as the 'heyday' of the show was clearly signposted. 'People have this kind of rosy image of vintage *Top of the Pops* of the sixties and seventies, and I wanted to re-create that,' he says. He commissioned a new theme tune, an updated version of the show's most famous theme, Led Zeppelin's 'Whole Lotta Love'. There was also a new logo, which incorporated the exclamation marks

from the original sixties logo. And the original introduction returned: now, each week before the titles, the presenters say, 'It's STILL Number One – it's *Top of the Pops*.'

Although Cowey didn't showcase the audience in the way the sixties directors had done, he still knew they were essential to the vibe. When he arrived, the age limit on the tickets said 15 and over, but it was clear that many of the audience were mature-looking 13-year-old girls in search of a boy band. 'The teenies were always a bit bemused by, say, Echo & the Bunnymen,' says warm-up man Danny Steggall. 'Ian McCulloch would be looking out over a front row of boob tubes and glittery eye shadow. When Chris moved it up to 18, it made a hell of a difference.' One artist who noticed that difference was Peter Andre, who returned briefly to the charts after an 18-month absence. He was used to getting

screams when he lifted his shirt to show his famous abs. Now, he got laughter.

The stars were still coming thick and fast, with pop bands like Boyzone, Steps and 5ive coming through and immediately hitting their stride. But no one better summed up the mood of the new *Top of the Pops* than Robbie Williams. A huge fan of the show, he'd even dropped in during the 'lost year' after he'd left Take That and was hanging around with Oasis. But in July 1996 he was back, performing his cover of George Michael's 'Freedom', triumphantly crashing back into the charts in his own right. Also on the show that week were The Spice Girls, Suede, Mark Morrison, and Bobby Brown with the re-formed New Edition.

Like the Spice Girls, Robbie continued to make himself available for *Top of the Pops* as his success grew and grew. And, like them, he

Above, left: Peter Andre, guest presenting the show on 9 August 1996. Robbie Williams made his solo debut that week, and the Spice Girls were at Number One with 'Wannabe'. Above, right: All Saints take it easy as they perform 'Never Ever'. They were the longest-lasting girl group to make it in the wake of the Spice Girls.

Above, left: 'Let Me Entertain You', says Robbie Williams in March 1998.
Above, right: Kylie Minogue meets Janet Jackson backstage at Elstree in 1998.

never failed to make an impact. For Robbie, being on the show was part of what defined being a pop star, and he always made some extra effort on the show – a special outfit, getting a girl up out of the audience and, on one occasion, famously dropping his trousers to reveal his tiger pants. In hindsight, though, he admits there was one mistake – the see-through gold dress he wore in August 1998 for 'Millennium'. 'That really wasn't me,' he confesses. 'I think I was going through a stage of "let's see how far I can push this". I think I went down a comedy cul-de-sac with that dress. And I couldn't find my way out.'

Cowey made regular presenters of Jamie Theakston, Jo Whiley, Zoe Ball and Jayne Middlemiss. 'It was quite an exciting time to be in there,' says Zoe. 'It was that kind of crossover period where there was a lot of pop around, but there were also some really good bands. And each week you'd be asking, "Who's on? Who's on?" ... And the audience is amazing. All the girls have massive boobs. I don't know what people are feeding their kids these days, but these girls in the audience – enormous boobs. They used to make me feel so inadequate.'

Top of the Pops covered the whole gamut of music in the late nineties – from Metallica to The Tweenies – apart from one area. A decade before, the new, 'faceless' dance music had created problems for the show. Now, there was a new breed of dance stars, acts like Prodigy, The Chemical Brothers, Underworld and Fatboy Slim, who were making a huge impact both in the UK and around the world. But they refused to do *Top of the Pops*. Being married to one of them (Fatboy Slim, aka Norman Cook), Zoe Ball has her own insight into why. 'It's difficult for DJs to do these things, because I

think they feel silly,' she says. 'That's the whole point of being a DJ, that you're behind the scenes, and a lot of them are uncomfortable with performing. I know my fella doesn't like the idea – they keep saying to him, "Will you do *Top of the Pops*?" and he's like, "What am I going to do?" ... I just think it looks really naff to have a DJ standing there on keyboards with a couple of dancers in front.'

Generally, though, the cast for *Top of the Pops* was getting better and better, particularly with the international acts for whom *Top of the Pops* became a regular stop-off as they made their whirlwind promotional tours around the globe. 'I produced the Brit Awards for a couple of years,' says Cowey, 'and that's such a massive event, with red carpet and limos. And sometimes I've been in the studio at *Top of the Pops* and thought, wow, we've got U2, Ricky Martin, Puff Daddy, Madonna – we've got the

best acts in the world. The Brits and the MTV Awards would struggle to come up with a line-up as good as we often have at *Top of the Pops*.' But of course these global acts wouldn't turn up if it wasn't worth their while. When *Top of the Pops* itself went global, around the turn of the new millennium, the show went to a new level. Then it really became worth their while.

Above, left: Gimme some Skin – Björk gave a one-off performance of her 1995 hit 'Army of Me' joined by Skin of Skunk Anansie.
Above, right: The Corrs pose for *Top of the Pops* magazine in the laundry at BBC Elstree.
Below: Jayne Middlemiss, Jo Whiley and Zoe Ball became regular presenters under new producer Chris Cowey.

JARVIS COCKER of Pulp was a regular performer on *Top of the Pops* from 1994 onwards. He also presented the show in October that year: 'It was my small contribution to modern culture', he says.

WHITNEY HOUSTON performing 'It's Not Right, But It's Okay' in a basque on the show in 1998.

108

RICKY MARTIN brought his own set to perform 'Livin' La Vida Loca' on *Top of the Pops*, the same set he'd used at the Grammy Awards.

CHER performing her Number One 'Believe' on *Top of the Pops* 33 years after she had appeared with Sonny Bono singing 'I Got You Babe'.

LIAM GALLAGHER of Oasis, caught in unusually pensive mood, on stage, during an instrumental break in their performance.

NOEL GALLAGHER singing an acoustic version of 'Sunday Morning Call' in a *Top of the Pops* special for BBC Music Live in Sheffield, May 2000.

THE SPICE GIRLS caught in the corridor at Elstree after their debut performance on *Top of the Pops* with 'Wannabe'.

WESTLIFE pose for a pin-up shot for *Top of the Pops* magazine. They also broke records as their first seven singles all debuted at Number One.

ALL SAINTS had a four-year run of hits and appearances on *Top of the Pops*, but their single 'Pure Shores' came second to Bob the Builder in the bestsellers of 2000.

PUFF DADDY, one of a string of American superstars to appear on the show in the late nineties, here performing 'PE 2000' in August 1999.

2000s

'*Top of the Pops* is a great British invention, like football and fish and chips,' says Chris Cowey, who by 2000 was executive producer. 'But when I first came to the show in the middle of '97, I was really surprised that it wasn't really exploited. It wasn't really seen anywhere else.'

The global dimension truly kicked in with the arrival of the new millennium, as the Corporation's commercial arm, BBC Worldwide, began to take more of an interest in the show. There had, of course, been a steady expansion in the 'exploitation' of the brand. *Top of the Pops* magazine was going from strength to strength, to be followed by a series of CDs, and a website. There were even two new versions of the show, *Top of the Pops Plus*, a Sunday lunchtime magazine show on BBC2 aimed at younger fans, and *Top of the Pops @ Play*, a live, three-hour request show on one of the BBC's digital ventures, UK Play. But this was just *Top of the Pops* moving with the times and keeping up with competition. The visionary step was to sell the show itself, the actual format, around the world.

At the end of the nineties, BBC Worldwide had huge success selling *Teletubbies* to almost every country. But each territory was encouraged to produce its own local version – for example, with locally shot films showing children at play. But when the same principle was applied to *Top of the Pops*, it became something that had never been attempted in television before. Countries were offered the chance to make *Top of the Pops* based on their own local charts. Local bands would perform on a set that was an exact replica of the one back at the BBC. This meant that international acts recorded in London could be cut into each local version, and it looked like they'd visited each country specially. It may be a simple idea but, technically, it's a huge feat because not only the set but also the lighting, the audience and even the way the show's directed all have to match. But when it works, it means that superstar acts like Destiny's Child or Ricky Martin need only record one *Top of the Pops* performance. First to get their own version of *Top of the Pops* were the Germans, soon to be followed by the Italians and the Dutch. By 2002 between 15 and 20 countries plan to

Above: Craig David.
Opposite, top to bottom:
Fran Healy of Travis;
Destiny's Child; S Club 7
at the *Top of the Pops*
Awards 2001.

Battle of the belly-
buttons.
Right: Jennifer Lopez at
the first *Top of the Pops*
Awards in Manchester.
Far right: Geri Halliwell's
dancers do as they're told
for the song 'Lift Me Up'.

have their own *Top of the Pops*, including the USA. The vision is that wherever an act may be in the world, they can drop in to their local *Top of the Pops* studio and their performance will be shown in every country. It's an incredibly well-oiled machine, but does create one curiosity. For the plan to work, the programme still has to be called *Top of the Pops* in each territory, leading to the strange phenomenon of German presenters exclaiming, 'Wer ist diese Woche *Top of the Pops*?'

The record companies, themselves so geared up towards global marketing, have been quick to take advantage of the international potential of *Top of the Pops*, knowing that a single performance can be used like a video to promote their acts in many different countries. During 2000 and 2001, they delivered acts of truly international stature to the bizarrely provincial environment of BBC Elstree. Madonna crowned a hugely successful year in 2000 with an appearance singing 'Music' and 'Don't Tell Me'. Other regulars have included Ricky Martin, U2, Jennifer

Lopez, Puff Daddy, Britney Spears, The Backstreet Boys, N*Sync, Destiny's Child, Janet Jackson, Marilyn Manson and Eminem.

Huge stars, of course, mean entourages: each of these acts seemed to want to outdo each other with the number of minders and hangers-on they brought with them. Undisputed champion of them all was Jennifer Lopez. For her spring 2001 appearance to promote her hits 'Play' and 'My Love Don't Cost A Thing', she had a personal guest list of 60 people. Her record company demanded 10 dressing rooms, which had to be redecorated and draped with white muslin. An orchid had to be placed in every room. Among the entourage were three chefs, who used one of the dressing rooms to prepare her hand-made ravioli and a choice of three Cuban desserts. When she rehearsed, all 60 of her 'peeps' went into the studio to applaud her mime. The wind-machine had to be operated by J-Lo's personal hairdresser, so that her hairdo would get blown about by exactly the right amount.

The crew, of course, smile sweetly at such excesses. But often, other stars raise an eyebrow or two. In 2000, The Artist Formerly Known As Prince arrived with a huge number of minders. He'd granted an interview to *Top of the Pops Plus*, which was to be recorded in the backstage green room. Naturally, his minders insisted that the room should be inspected and cleared out – just as Robbie Williams had decided he wanted to relax in there. Robbie took offence at being kicked out of the back-stage area, and when he went on to perform, he announced to the audience, 'Tonight I'm going to kick somebody's head in like it's 1999.'

Moments like this are fully in keeping with Chris Cowey's vision that the show should be an 'event' every single week, like the Brits or the MOBOs, and central to that idea was to have the show in a venue. In the middle of 2001, *Top of the Pops* was evicted from the Elstree home it had occupied for 10 years, to make room for the ever-expanding *EastEnders*, which was going to be shown four nights a week. Cowey worked hard to find a suitable location for *Top of the Pops*, and for seven months, its home was the Riverside Studios made famous by Chris Evans and *TFI Friday*, which had recently ended. However, the BBC weren't having any of it. *Top of the Pops* was now a prestige show, and they wanted it back home at Television Centre.

Cowey's intuition was always to work outside of the corporate control that had tended to interfere with *Top of the Pops* over the years, but he was overruled. He wasn't exactly dragged kicking and screaming to Television Centre, but he demanded a high price. He requested a bigger budget, a spectacular new set, and a backstage 'Star Bar' area where celebs and artists could hang out and look glamorous during the links. It would be like the sixties again, but this time the glitterati would be on

screen. He got everything he asked for, and on 19 October 2001 the new-look *Top of the Pops* was launched with an hour-long show on BBC1, amid much celebration. Even the show's original presenter, Sir Jimmy Savile, turned up to give his seal of approval, and to introduce a live performance by U2.

The summer of 2002 sees another land-mark for *Top of the Pops* – one with which this book is published to coincide – the 2000th edition. The view from within Chris Cowey's team is excited and optimistic. The show's well ahead of the competition and the weekly parade of fantastic acts never seems to stop. In Los Angeles, a set is being built as an exact replica of the one in London, which will play host to even more superstars, whose perform-ances will be seen on US network TV, as well as back home on the BBC. But in light of what's emerged from this book, there are ele-ments of the story which never change. There's still a feeling that the BBC itself doesn't really understand the show, and that *Top of the Pops* is seen as an unruly brat that the bosses don't quite know what to do with.

The music, though, will always be there, and that's the secret to the show's success. So there are no better words to end with than those of the man who saved the show from the BBC in the early nineties, Ric Blaxill. He says, 'You can never underestimate how important music is to everyday life, what songs and artists actually mean to people. Everybody has grown up liking music, loving particular bands and artists, and *Top of The Pops* is that unique show where once a week you can sit down and see all these people that you adore – or maybe you don't, maybe you hate them. But music will always create some kind of reaction, and there will always be new music coming along, and that's why *Top of the Pops* will always be there.'

Above: Marilyn Manson's performance of 'Beautiful People' was so scary that it could only be shown on the late-night *Top of the Pops*.

JENNIFER LOPEZ needed one of the biggest entourages ever seen at the show when she appeared to record 'Play' and 'My Love Don't Cost A Thing'.

JANET JACKSON shows off the best stomach muscles seen on *Top of the Pops* since Peter Andre, as she sings her 2001 hit, 'Because of You'.

EMINEM's July 2000 performance of his Number One single, 'The Real Slim Shady', was deemed too controversial for primetime, and could only be shown in the late-night repeat.

U2 chose a 'Beautiful Day' to set up on the roof of their own hotel, the Clarence in Dublin, to record especially for the show in 2001.

ROBBIE WILLIAMS drops his trousers to show off his famous tiger pants for the song 'Rock DJ', prompting over 150 complaints to the BBC.

BRITNEY SPEARS brought dozens of her own staff to Television Centre in January 2002 for her performance of 'Overprotected'.

acknowledgements

This book is based on the BBC1 documentary *Top of the Pops: The True Story*, broadcast on 1 January 2001. My first thanks go to Eliot 'Fight for the Right to Party' Johnson, who co-produced the programme with me, and to our executive producers Mark 'Mysterious Ways' Cooper and Chris 'Don't Stop the Rock' Cowey. Also, to researchers Sophie 'Supersonic' Waite, Shelly 'Belfast Child' Lowrey and Clare 'Bette Davis Eyes' Lucas. Special thanks also to Alan 'Uncle Kracker' Fitzjohn, guardian of the *Top of the Pops* archive, and to the dozens of people who have worked at *Top of the Pops* past and present who helped me, including Stan 'Daddy Cool' Dorfman, Danny 'Firestarter' Steggall, Flick 'Dancing Queen' Colby, Ruth 'Three Times A Lady' Pearson and Mark 'A Little Bit Country' Hagan. Thanks also to the many artists, producers, dancers and record-company staff who gave interviews. The pictures in this book are by many different photographers, but the work of Harry 'Girls on Film' Goodwin in the sixties and seventies, and of Mark 'Life Through A Lens' Allan in recent years deserve particular praise and thanks. This book is for my friend, Odilon 'Little Star' Rocha: *Nao esqueca dos seus sonhos*.

index

picture credits

BBC Worldwide would like to thank the following for permission to reproduce copyright material. While every effort has been made to trace and acknowledge all copyright holders, we would like to apologize for any errors or omissions.

Associated Press page 21; IDOLS 94 (Philip Ollerenshaw); LFI 93 (Kristin Callahan), 36t; Rex Features 13, 49.

All other photos © BBC with thanks to:
Mark Allan 90t, 98r, 100, 103r, 104, 105b, 107–11, 114–25; Jo Cook 24; Harry Goodwin 9, 14, 17, 20t, 24t, 25t, 26–35, 38, 42bl, 52–5; *Radio Times*/Don Smith 5, 8 main, 22, 23, 65, 75r, 102, 103l;

Top of the Pops magazine 96, 101, 105tl, 106 (Ray Burmiston), 112, 113 (Neil Cooper), 105tr (Jamie Fry), 90b (Mike Prior); Anthony Wood 15b, 68t, 70t; © BBC 62t, 73 (Barry Boxall), 77r, 88 (John Jefford), 70b, 74, 76, 77l, 78 (Philip Taylor), 72b (Spike Watson).